YOUTH AND COMMUNITY EMPOWERMENT IN EUROPE

Peter Evans and Angelika Krüger

First published in Great Britain in 2013 by

Policy Press
University of Bristol
6th Floor
Howard House
Queen's Avenue
Clifton
Bristol BS8 1SD
UK
Tel +44 (0)117 331 5020
Fax +44 (0)117 331 5367
e-mail pp-info@bristol.ac.uk
www.policypress.co.uk

North American office:
Policy Press
c/o The University of Chicago Press
1427 East 60th Street
Chicago, IL 60637, USA
t: +1 773 702 7700
f: +1 773-702-9756
e:sales@press.uchicago.edu
www.press.uchicago.edu

© Policy Press 2013

British Library Cataloguing in Publication Data
A catalogue record for this book is available from the British Library

Library of Congress Cataloging-in-Publication Data
A catalog record for this book has been requested

ISBN 978 1 44730 592 7 paperback

The right of Peter Evans and Angelika Krüger to be identified as authors of this work has been asserted by them in accordance with the 1988 Copyright, Designs and Patents Act.

Cover design by Qube Design Associates, Bristol
Front cover: image kindly supplied by www.istock.com
Printed in Great Britain by www.4edge.co.uk

For the YEPP Community, all our friends and colleagues who are committed to youth and community empowerment and social change through civic engagement.

Contents

List of figures and tables

Figures

Tables

Abbreviations

ABCD	asset-based community development
CERI	Centre for Educational Research and Innovation
CIPP	context, input, process, product
EFC	European Foundation Centre
ICE	Institute for Community Education
ICON	Inner City Organisations Network
INA	International Academy at the Free University of Berlin
IRC	International Resource Centre
NEF	Network of European Foundations for Innovative Cooperation
NEIC	North East Inner City (Dublin)
OECD	Organisation for Economic Co-operation and Development
PYME	Participatory YEPP Monitoring and Evaluation Design
RISO	Antwerp's centre for community development
YEPP	Youth Empowerment Partnership Programme
YPAR	Young People at Risk

Acknowledgements

The authors would like to thank the Charles Stewart Mott Foundation for a grant that made the preparation of this book possible. They would like to thank the members of the YEPP programme teams, in particular Mr Peter Bleckmann, Dr Cordula Strocka and Dr Tetiana Katsbert as well as Ms Leanna Eaton, Ms Steffi Leupold, Mr Paul Duke, Mr Kim Sandstrom and Mr Victor Fleurot.

They would also like to thank the local researchers who provided regular reports and assessments for the internal evaluation of YEPP I; and the evaluation facilitators and local coordinators who have implemented the participatory YEPP monitoring and evaluation approach in YEPP II and who wrote the portraits of the YEPP Local Programme Sites. They all contributed to the analysis of the Youth Empowerment Partnership Programme and the reflection on youth and community empowerment in Europe.

Preface

The alienation experienced by young people living in areas of severe social disadvantage throughout Europe presents challenges that are as complex as they are urgent. Increasing numbers of children and young people across Europe are facing severe risks of social exclusion.

Social exclusion is one of the most pressing challenges for modern societies, both in Europe and globally. As a report issued by the Youth Research Partnership of the Council of Europe and the European Commission states, there is a consensus among researchers that 'social exclusion includes political and cultural dimensions as well as economic poverty. It combines linked problems which typically accumulate […] and it is a dynamic process which occurs over time' (Colley et al, 2005, in Bleckmann and Krüger, 2007, p 7). This understanding acknowledges the fact that socially excluded individuals are often facing simultaneously a range of interwoven problems. At the beginning of the 21st century, the risk of social exclusion in many European countries has grown from a problem limited to distinct groups of people to a phenomenon that is affecting growing numbers of citizens from diverse backgrounds, including formerly middle-class families and neighbourhoods. There are of course groups who continue to be particularly vulnerable and for whom social exclusion – in its diverse forms – is a reality of their daily lives; yet, the risks of social exclusion are no longer limited to these minorities.

Children and young people in particular are facing growing risks of social exclusion; the challenges they have to cope with in their biographies have become more fragmented, complex and contradictory. For instance, from the socioeconomic side of exclusion, young people are among the groups that are most vulnerable to income poverty. Data derived from broad quantitative surveys (Aassve et al, 2006) clearly indicate that, although each individual country may differ in its general approach to social welfare and in its economic strength, the problem of child and youth poverty is remarkably consistent right across Europe. Even young people who have been successful in accessing the labour market are often denied decent labour. Insecure and precarious employment constellations are typical phenomena that have a direct impact on the lives of young people. As the Barrow Cadbury Trust has found, 'Even when young people seek to improve their employment prospects, there is little evidence that participation in training schemes, further education courses and work preparation programmes – and the qualifications they gain – help their chances of getting and staying in rewarding, secure jobs' (Webster et al, 2005, in Bleckmann and Krüger, 2007, p 7). As a consequence, young people today are increasingly experiencing an extended phase of 'yo-yo transitions' (Walter and Pohl, 2005, p 155) instead of systematic pathways from a relatively insecure youth to a relatively stable adulthood. This experience is affecting large numbers of young Europeans throughout their transition to adulthood.

Socioeconomic problems do not exist in a vacuum; they are intricately linked with political and cultural dimensions of exclusion and disintegration. German researchers argue that these dimensions include 'problems of participation; the meaninglessness of everyday politics as experienced by many people; [...] unstable community affiliations combined with a lack of real emotional recognition' (The Institute for Interdisciplinary Research on Conflict and Violence, 2002–2005, p 1). Few young people see themselves as empowered enough to express their views in public, to have an impact on political decision-making and to contribute to positive changes in society. As a report from the Youth Empowerment Partnership Programme (YEPP) states, 'The fear of losing control, of a fading identity plays a major role in many of nowadays' most dangerous social developments, such as nationalist or religious fanaticism, violence, and exclusion' (Bleckmann, 2004, p 20).

As a result of complex experiences of social exclusion, there is a growing frustration among young people because they are not being given fair and just opportunities. This feeling is compounded when experiences of discrimination (because of ethnic or cultural background, gender, disabilities, or sexual orientation) are added to the general challenges already mentioned. The riots in Paris and other European cities in 2005 and those in England in 2011 are especially striking incidents indicating these developments. The problems leading to this outbreak of violence continue to exist, and they appear in other forms in communities throughout Europe. For example, the number of European young people attracted by anti-democratic groups and ideologies, including authoritarian, racist, or radical religious groups and movements, is growing and, while the factors leading to such attitudes and actual participation are complex and diverse, promises of recognition, social cohesion and an offer of clear roles and tasks for those who participate seem to contribute to the attractiveness of anti-democratic groups. It is this manifest desire and willingness on the part of young people to want to influence decision-making linked to the creation of their own futures that must be engaged to renew and increase their involvement in the democratic process and reduce the frustrations that many of them are increasingly experiencing in mainstream democratic societies.

Social exclusion directly affects the individual lives of young people: yet, it would be short-sighted to view these challenges as individual problems only. Following a rights-based approach – in accordance with the UN Convention of the Rights of the Child (1990) – Evans et al (2000) argue that the social exclusion of young people should be understood as an indicator of intrinsic societal problems if a society does not respect their basic rights by, for example, presenting obstacles to the progress of individuals and even to citizenship. The implications of this view are that social exclusion could be argued to exist in most areas of modern living, including education, employment, community life and citizenship.

These societal deficiencies affect the daily lives of Europe's young people; they are experiencing a lack of recognition and social coherence in their immediate local environments, with the creation of the European Union making the situation even more complex.[1] However, the extent to which communities are affected by the risks of social exclusion vary considerably: social exclusion 'is not randomly distributed, but concentrated spatially in disadvantaged neighbourhoods' (see Colley et al, 2005, p 9). To combat young people's social exclusion, therefore, it is critical to contribute to systemic changes within the most disadvantaged communities, in order to strengthen their capacity to provide more supportive environments for children and young people.

Increasingly, the need for preventive, community-based and holistic responses to social exclusion has entered the public debate, but concerted action and policies that respect these principles are still more the exception than the rule. Such proactive approaches have the potential both to strengthen the individual young people and to support the regeneration of the communities in which they live. By contrast, traditional responses to the social exclusion of children and young people have typically been interventions which are mobilised in response to very visible problems of exclusion and disadvantage – which means that resources are invested at a very late stage and are often struggling to react only to the more obvious symptoms of more deeply entrenched societal problems. Further, traditional, piecemeal approaches can largely be characterised by a lack of integration: 'yet another training course' is created whenever a specific problem is identified, without a thorough analysis of how already existing resources and programmes could be pooled and integrated, and how the existing systems of education, social and health services, as well as urban planning, should be transformed in order to contribute to and support positive change.

Another key aspect to overcoming social exclusion is the role that is attributed to those affected by exclusion: are they seen as mere victims who are in need of public assistance, or are they viewed as potential protagonists who, if given the opportunity, are capable of contributing to positive change both for themselves and for their community? As Amartya Sen asked: are they 'patients or agents' (Sen, 1999)? Sustainable change has to be brought about by the people themselves. The views and experiences of socially excluded groups must be taken into account from the outset. This requires, on the one hand, changing the systems of decision making in order to create more opportunities for stakeholder involvement and active participation; and, on the other hand, additional efforts in systematic capacity building and training of community members in order to establish and hone the skills that are necessary for contributing to positive change.

Worldwide experience in the field of youth and community development suggests that the limited impact of the traditional, piecemeal approaches can only be overcome through:

• interdisciplinary and integrated approaches;
• pooling expertise, experiences and resources of the public, private, and the independent sectors;
• developing joint actions and working in partnership across boundaries, based on shared values and goals;
• holistic, community-based and needs-based approaches;
• influencing local public service structures, relevant legal regulations and policies in the field of youth and community development.

Only such a comprehensive, multi-faceted approach to community development is capable of achieving integrated, holistic and sustainable change in the lives of individuals and in the communities most affected by social exclusion. Recently, some public as well as independent programmes have been created at local, national and European levels that are coordinating approaches and facilitating multi-agency strategies, allowing for public service delivery to meet more systematically the needs of their clients. However, while such programmes are a positive step forward and have gained recognition in some European countries, a comprehensive, multi-faceted approach to community development is far from central to mainstream European policy-making.

This is the broader context in which YEPP has been developed and implemented. This context is a necessary foundation in order to understand YEPP and its model of change. The programme design is community-based and has taken into account the principles of cross-sectoral cooperation, empowerment and participation in order to achieve systemic and sustainable change in the lives of young people and the communities in which they live.

Foundation interest in community programmes

During the 20th century, many foundations started developing community-oriented programmes, some of which have been influenced by the community development approach. What has made the approach attractive for foundations is the value system on which it is based and the emphasis on active citizenship. This was in line with the move that many foundations made from a more welfare-oriented approach towards a more active and participatory approach. This may have also been a natural progression because many foundations have strong roots in specific locations, and very often this has contributed to their wish to enhance the living conditions in a particular geographical area. Having gathered local experience, many foundations have also made efforts to transfer their successes to other contexts and places. As independent funders, foundations depend on the collaboration and support of different agencies from various sectors in order to be efficient, and are less likely to be bound to traditional structures and departmental divisions – factors which sometimes inhibit substantial innovations within the public sector. As a result, foundations have the chance to initiate programmes in a slightly more flexible and innovative way. Several foundation programmes and initiatives from many countries have informed the approach of YEPP.

For instance, since the 1990s, the Annie E. Casey Foundation has invested in different multi-year community development programmes, such as the 'Transforming Neighbourhoods' and 'Making Connections' programmes. The 'Making Connections' programme (Annie E. Casey, 2010) is a multi-year programme in 40 deprived communities across the United States, based on the conviction that:

> by themselves neither employment projects nor school improvement efforts nor community organising activities will likely prove sufficient to reverse the negative trajectory of the environments for families in our toughest communities. Rather, what is required is an unprecedented intense, extended and comprehensive commitment to address the array of forces that are unravelling so many inner-city

neighbourhoods [...] Moreover such a commitment – to be earnest – will require an ambitious and lasting partnership among state and local officials, neighbourhood residents and leaders, employers and investors, and leaders of local philanthropic and non-profit communities. (Annie E. Casey Foundation, 1997, in Bleckmann and Krüger, 2007, p 16)

As a foundation initiative, this programme inspired the design of YEPP and became a role model because so much emphasis was given to local leadership and decision making: 'Rather than imposing a specific agenda, we hope to nurture and support local movements dedicated to improving neighbourhood conditions' (Annie E. Casey Foundation, 1998–99, in Bleckmann and Krüger, 2007, pp 16–17).

Many of the foundations that are active in the YEPP network have long-standing experience in the areas of youth and community development and community education. These include, for instance, the Charles Stewart Mott Foundation (US), the Ford Foundation (US), the Freudenberg Foundation (Germany) and the Robert Bosch Foundation (Germany).

Theory and Concept of Change

YEPP's Theory and Concept of Change was inspired by these experiences and by the community development and community education movements at local and international levels. In addition, YEPP's specific approach was informed through the success of public-private partnership, by the international discussion and implementation of empowerment strategies and the action research approach. Furthermore, the lessons learnt from public programmes for urban regeneration were reflected and taken into account.

Although some of the main features were already clear from the outset, YEPP's Theory and Concept of Change has developed dynamically throughout the implementation and evaluation phase of the programme, and it continues to be discussed by all those involved in YEPP. In this sense, the following outline indicates the outcome of an on-going developmental process.

The development of this Theory and Concept of Change has been inspired by the reflections of the International Network for Strategic Philanthropy (INSP), which has published both theoretical reflections and practical toolkits for foundations interested in developing and explicating their theories of change:

> The goal is to enable foundations to think more clearly about their assumptions and to make better informed choices. The sort of tool we have in mind would identify key questions for foundations, including: What do we want to achieve? What is the nature of the problem we want to address/change? Who or what needs to change? In what ways? How could we achieve that change? What assets do we have to apply to that? What externally or internally imposed constraints are we operating under? (Leat, 2005, in Bleckmann and Krüger, 2007, p 32)

YEPP has set out to establish an innovative European and transatlantic cooperation and partnership of foundations in order to share and combine their expertise in the fields of children and youth, education, community development and civil society. Through their collaboration, they intend to transfer and replicate best practices and to create new initiatives with cooperating foundations/corporate funders, European institutions and the local and national public sectors in the participating programme sites. These new initiatives are taking place in a range of domains, including educational (formal/non-formal), economic, cultural, political and social areas. Through establishing public-private partnerships at local, regional, national and European levels, the partners of YEPP wish to contribute to overcoming the fragmentation of public and private initiatives and services. Their intention is to inform relevant policy debates and to influence public as well as independent and private programming.

The ultimate goal of these initiatives is to support the empowerment of youth at risk and the environment in which young people live by:

- increasing young people's choices and their opportunities to actively participate in their local communities and societies at large;
- overcoming young people's exclusion from full participation in society and reducing risk factors;
- overcoming disadvantage and discrimination and supporting young people's equal opportunities, regardless of their background;
- activating the local resources to create more supportive and inclusive environments for young people and the community members at large.

Taking into account worldwide experiences in the fields of youth and community development, YEPP's partners agree on a number of basic assumptions about how long-term changes benefiting disadvantaged children, young people and their families can be brought about. These are:

- Young people experience the positive and negative influences of society most directly in the local communities in which they live. This is where they go to school, where they develop the major part of their social relationships, where they come into contact with public services and where they experience what society has to offer. Positive or negative economic trends as well as successful or failing public policies all play out in the local communities. *Therefore, interventions to support young people's empowerment must start at community level and involve key local actors in the change process.*
- Young people at risk face a number of problems and challenges regarding their personal, social, political, economic and cultural development. Fragmented approaches will not create the required conditions to empower young people. *Instead, youth empowerment can be supported best by holistic approaches that respond in a coordinated way to the challenges young people face in their daily lives.*
- Many youth projects have been created in response to a perceived crisis, and thus try to respond to a specific problem (for example, unemployment) by short-term interventions. Many of these projects have not been integrated into other services and have failed to achieve sustainable change after the project has been terminated. *Achieving long-term change for youth empowerment requires long-term planning and coordinated efforts across sectors and departments.*
- Change is brought about by people themselves and therefore depends on the capabilities of individuals. However, in order to achieve greater impact and long-term change, well-functioning organisations are also needed as frameworks for local self-organisation. *Change can be facilitated best by strengthening the capacities of key actors, including youth themselves, and by supporting the development of local civil society organisations and providing a framework for active participation.*
- Sustainable change requires an understanding of the various relationships within the community and the causes of disempowerment and exclusion. For new structures to be effective, stakeholders must understand the issues through direct experience at the local level. *Change needs authentic knowledge – and people who and organisations which are prepared to draw conclusions from that knowledge when planning actions for change.*
- YEPP's partners seek fundamental and long-term improvements for young people experiencing disadvantage and exclusion. *Such*

improvements require changes to the systems and policies that affect at-risk youth and the communities in which they live.

Note

[1] The European Union (EU) has led to an abundance of international opportunities for those citizens who are successful. For those who are not, there are few, thus creating a 'citizenship divide'. YEPP has been called the 'Erasmus Programme' for the disadvantaged. The Erasmus Programme provides opportunities for EU university students to study in different member states of the EU.

Background to the Youth Empowerment Partnership Programme

This book provides an up-to-date account of the first decade of the Youth Empowerment Partnership Programme (YEPP) (2001–11). In 2012 YEPP entered a new era, and although 'YEPP', as an approach and methodology, continues to be implemented in YEPP Local Sites, the organisational structure and governance at an international level have taken a different form from the first decade. As a result, the authors prefer to use the past tense in this section when referring to YEPP I and YEPP II.

YEPP was supported by a consortium of European and American foundations and aims to improve the quality of life of young people living in disadvantaged communities through their empowerment and active participation in their local communities and societies at large. YEPP originated within the Youth and Education Interest Group of the European Foundation Centre (EFC) in 1998 following a commissioned review of Foundations' 'Youth funding and policies' in Europe and the US by Krüger and Picht (1999). The Network of European Foundations for Innovative Cooperation (NEF) provided the legal framework for the programme. The European Foundation Centre (EFC) in which YEPP 'was born' has remained as a supportive partner for making contacts with foundations and international organisations.

YEPP was overseen by a Steering Committee whose principal members were representatives of the contributing Foundations, the International Academy for Innovative Pedagogy, Psychology and Economics (INAgGmbH) of the Free University of Berlin and NEF. Permanent observers were the EFC and, from 2002 to 2008, the representative from the Centre for Educational Research and Innovation of the Organisation for Economic Cooperation and Development (OECD/CERI).

As of 2011, the partner foundations of YEPP and members of the Steering Committee were: Barrow Cadbury Trust, Charles Stewart Mott Foundation (Vice Chair), Compagnia di San Paolo (Chair), Evens Foundation, Foundation Bernheim and the Irish Youth Foundation.

Since the beginning of 2012, three of the former partner foundations are providing start-up funding for the new era of YEPP: Barrow

Cadbury Trust, Charles Stewart Mott Foundation, and Compagnia di San Paolo.

As of 2011, the Foundations involved in YEPP programme sites were: Compagnia di San Paolo (all Italian sites); Evens Foundation (Antwerp North, Belgium and Warszawa Bielany, Poland); ERSTE Stiftung (Košice, Slovakia); Fondazione Cassa di Risparmio della Spezia (La Spezia, Italy); Fondazione Cassa di Risparmio di Cuneo (Langhe, Italy); Community Foundation Savonese (Albenga and Loano, Italy); Freudenberg Stiftung and Charles Stewart Mott Foundation (Community Foundation Tuzla; Bosnia and Herzegovina); and the Irish Youth Foundation (Dublin North East Inner City, Ireland).

The majority of the Foundations continue with their support at local level in the new era of YEPP, including: Charles Stewart Mott Foundation, Compagnia di San Paolo, ERSTE Stiftung, Fondazione Cassa di Risparmio della Spezia, Fondazione Cassa di Risparmio di Cuneo, and Freudenberg Stiftung.

The first two phases of YEPP

The first phase of the programme, YEPP I, took place over the period 2002–06 in seven Local Programme Sites in six European countries. The second, YEPP II, was expanded to include 18 Local Programme Sites in eight European countries. YEPP helps communities to empower themselves and their citizens by creating partnerships between the independent, public and private sectors and young people in Local Support Groups. Each Local Support Group identifies aims and goals and a means to achieve them, and evaluates progress.

YEPP I was a research phase that carefully followed progress in the seven Local Programme Sites over a period of three years during its implementation. The main part of the book is based on data gathered during this period via internal and external evaluations. YEPP II continued the YEPP I work. It used the same model of implementation as YEPP I but introduced a participatory monitoring and evaluation concept with no external evaluation, and in this sense it was more of a development than a research programme. The new era of YEPP continues with the approach established during YEPP II. An account of YEPP II and additional information on a number of Local Programme Sites is provided in Chapters Five and Six. General conclusions and an outline on the future of YEPP are supplied in Chapter Seven.

Figure 1: Map of YEPP Local Programme Sites as of May 2011

A transnational platform and network of 18 local programme sites in 8 European countries

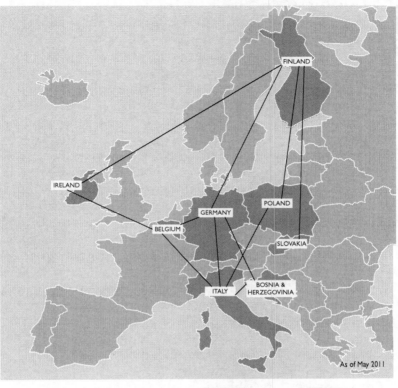

IRELAND
Dublin North
Inner City
ITALY
Turin-Mirafiori
Albenga
Genoa-Cornigliano
Loano
La Spezia
Langhe
Turin 'The Gate' (affiliate site)

BELGIUM
Antwerp-North
SLOVAKIA
Kecerovce-Olšava

FINLAND
Kristinestad
Kimitoön
Väståboland
GERMANY
Görlitz

POLAND
Warsaw-Bielany
Zgorzelec

**BOSNIA AND
HERZEGOVINA**
Tuzla-Simin Han
Gornja Tuzla

The results show that YEPP works and could form part of a new solution for tackling issues related to the exclusion of many young people from the European project. It gives them a central role in the reconstruction of the communities in which they live by putting more power and opportunity into their hands and through close collaboration with the public, private and independent sectors.

The role of foundations

YEPP was initiated by a group of independent foundations working together to create new models of partnership to support young people living in disadvantaged areas across Europe. This has proved to be visionary in the light of new public policies to include civil society more extensively that are emerging following the economic crash of 2007–08. The investment in a research programme to provide valid and reliable data on the effectiveness of YEPP should also be able to have a strong impact on policy-making, where evidence for effectiveness is ever more required.

By the time of the beginning of YEPP II, some partner foundations had left YEPP, mainly those that did not believe in long-term commitment, but new partner foundations had come on board. The general programme budget was covered by the consortium of foundations. Additional funds had to be raised for non-recurring activity costs. Main donors have been foundations and the European Commission, in particular the Directorate-General for Education and Culture, Youth in Action Programme.

The authors and the YEPP community are indebted to the following foundations for the continued support that they have given to, and the faith that they have shown in YEPP. They are:

- Charles Stewart Mott Foundation, USA (since 2001);
- Compagnia di San Paolo, Italy (since 2002);
- Evens Foundation, Belgium (since 2001);
- Foundation Bernheim, Belgium (since 2001);
- Ford Foundation, USA (2004–2008);
- Freudenberg Foundation, Germany (2001–2010);
- Irish Youth Foundation, Ireland (2001–2010);
- The Foundation for Swedish Culture in Finland (2001–2005);
- Barrow Cadbury Trust, UK (since 2008).

Other foundations that have also contributed to YEPP include:

- Atlantic Philanthropies, Ireland;
- ERSTE Foundation, Austria;
- European Cultural Foundation, Netherlands;
- German Children and Youth Foundation, Germany;
- Hertie Foundation, Germany;
- King Baudouin Foundation, Belgium;

- King's Fund, UK;
- Robert Bosch Foundation, Germany.

Programme partners

From the inception of YEPP, INAgGmbH and OECD/CERI were key partners and collaborators.[1] From the late 1980s up to 2007, concerns about the economic consequences of social exclusion and the under-performance of students, threatening their employability, led OECD/CERI to carry out studies on 'children and youth at risk' (OECD, 1995). Immediately before being involved in YEPP, CERI had completed a report on 'Coordinating Services for children and youth at risk' (OECD, 1998) that was partly funded by the Charles Stewart Mott Foundation. YEPP was a natural follow-up to this work, and the continuing involvement of OECD/CERI was supported by the member countries of the OECD/CERI and in part by the foundations involved in YEPP. This partnership continued until 2008 when CERI's programme of work changed.

In addition, the INAgGmbH housed the YEPP I and II Programme Team, comprising the Programme Director, two Programme Officers and a Programme Assistant. This situation is continuing in the new era of YEPP with INAgGmbH also taking on the administrative responsibilities for YEPP previously carried by the Network of European Foundations for Innovative Cooperation (NEF). NEF held the legal responsibility for YEPP I and II and was a supportive partner for making and maintaining contacts with foundations and European organisations.

YEPP also actively includes and depends on a wide range of partner organisations at local, national and European levels that share an interest in promoting youth empowerment. In particular, municipalities play a significant role in the local communities where YEPP works. Finally, of critical importance to YEPP is the active participation within the programme of young people and other citizens from the local communities across Europe where YEPP is currently working.

Funding

Although YEPP has been strongly and faithfully supported by the partner foundations over a number of years, the annual costs of the programme are not high in comparison, for instance, to those of the Annie E. Casey Foundation's work, Making Connections (Annie E. Casey, 2010), which runs into tens of millions of US dollars.

Each involved foundation made a minimum annual contribution of €15,000 for the overall programme budget plus the external evaluation. Four foundations made substantially larger contributions of up to €150,000 per annum.

In the first phase of YEPP, foundations also supported the appointment of local coordinators and local researchers in the sites where YEPP was taking place, at an average cost of €40,000 per annum. In the second phase of YEPP, in some cases these costs were covered by the local municipalities. In addition, foundations invested between €20,000 and €100,000 per annum for activity costs such as local projects and events.

Costs for the transnational component were also separately covered by specific grants from individual foundations and the European Union (EU).

The OECD/CERI also made contributions in kind, through providing permanent full-time staff members and facilities such as meeting rooms. OECD/CERI also reported on the work to all of its member countries.

INA contributed in kind by hosting the YEPP programme office, with four full-time staff members.

The following organisations have provided additional funding for YEPP between 2001 and 2011.

2001
- EU DG Employment and Social Affairs ('Overcoming Fragmentation – New Forms of Partnership in Combating and Preventing Social Exclusion')

2004
- Ford Foundation (Support for YEPP Community Conference January 2005 and March 2006 + Capacity Building Workshop November 2005; Ford Foundation became a partner and member of the YEPP Steering Committee)

2007
- Ford Foundation (Support for YEPP II)

2008
- Barrow Cadbury Trust (Support for general purpose grant for YEPP. The Barrow Cadbury Trust became a partner and member of the YEPP Steering Committee)
- Atlantic Philanthropies (Successful application for YEPP Community Conference in Dublin, June 2008)

2009
- EU DG Education and Culture – Youth in Action Programme: Action 4.6 – Partnerships ('Inspiring Youth to Act – Partnerships for the Empowerment and Active Citizenship of Young People with Fewer Opportunities')
- Robert Bosch Stiftung (Support for the establishment of a YEPP Programme Site in Görlitz, Germany, and Zgorzelec, Poland)
- ERSTE Stiftung (Support to establish a YEPP Programme Site in Kosice, Slovakia, with special focus on Roma inclusion)

2010
- EU DG Education and Culture – Youth in Action Programme: Actions 5.1

2011
- ERSTE Stiftung (second grant for YEPP Programme Site in Slovakia)
- EU DG Education and Culture – Youth in Action Programme: Actions 5.1

Note

[1] The OECD (Organisation for Economic Co-operation and Development) is an international organisation comprising 32 of the wealthiest countries in the world. Through international comparisons and analysis it provides policy advice to the governments of its member countries on all aspects of their work. The CERI (Centre for Educational Research and Innovation), which is part of the Directorate for Education, carries out policy-related research on educational matters within the context of the OECD.

ONE

Introduction: the theoretical context of the YEPP approach

The Youth Empowerment Partnership Programme (YEPP) supports young people and the communities in which they live by increasing their self-organising and self-determining capabilities through a process of individual and local empowerment brought about through the creation of partnerships. The thinking lying behind YEPP depends on two major movements – the community development approach and community education. A very brief overview of these two movements is provided in the following paragraphs, based on Bleckmann and Krüger (2007).

The community development approach

The community development approach is a participatory and people-empowering model, aimed at increasing peoples' capacity to influence the conditions which affect their lives. It has been developed as a response to the widespread problems of disempowerment and social exclusion that are characteristic of modern societies. The approach is dedicated to improving local conditions, especially for people living in disadvantaged contexts; it introduces a shift of paradigm by redefining the community and the role it plays in shaping its own conditions and environment and in determining change. The goal is to regenerate community and re-establish active citizenship. As a professional practice of working and learning together with local individuals and groups, this approach supports and encourages people to become active agents or protagonists, rather than passive recipients of developments and change.

While the community development approach has a long history going back to the 19th century (for instance, Owen, 1813), more recently it has seen a resurgence of interest in many countries. In the US and the UK, for instance, 'community organising' re-emerged in the 1980s. It has been defined as a values-based process by which people – most often low- and moderate-income people previously with no access to decision-making processes – are brought together in civil society organisations or spontaneous informal action groups to act jointly in the interest of their communities and the common good. Ideally, in the participatory process of working for needed change, citizens who are involved in community-organising groups learn how to take greater responsibility for the future of their communities, make their voices heard and achieve growth as individuals.

The concepts had also been developed in other European countries, for example in Germany, called '*Gemeinwesenarbeit*', and in the Flemish part of Belgium, as '*Buurtwerk*' and have influenced other programmes developed in Europe in the second half of the 20th century, such as the 'Contrats de Ville' and the 'Développement Social des Quartiers' in France and the 'Soziale Stadt' programme in Germany. At the end of the 1980s, the fall of the Berlin Wall and the collapse of the communist regimes in Central and Eastern Europe, these countries opened the way for the emergence of community development in this part of Europe.

At the outset, these programmes focused on the renewal of infrastructure and the physical environment, which proved too narrow an approach. What was missing was the human factor, which, when addressed through social and economic initiatives that empowered people in the communities, led to greater success (Strandberg, 2001). This realisation pointed to the need for developing multi-level programmes in order to attack the multi-causal problems experienced in disadvantaged communities.

In the late 1990s and early 2000s, several initiatives were established to explore the potential contributions of young people to community development. For example, the 'Youth Leadership for Development', which was created in the US in 1999 by the Innovation Centre for Community and Youth Development and supported by the Ford Foundation, explored how young people benefit from social activism. In the evaluation of this initiative it was concluded that:

> civic activism is a powerful approach for reaching youth who are often not reached by conventional youth programmes, because civic activism provides a forum for youth to reflect on and address the day-to-day challenges faced by their families and communities, and because civic activism provides applied vocational and leadership opportunities (The Innovation Center for Community and Youth. Development, 2007, in Bleckmann and Krüger, 2007, p 18)

The Positive Youth Development Approach developed by Karen Pittman is based on a vision of young people as potential protagonists, rather than as welfare recipients. This approach has been successfully implemented by the International Youth Foundation and its partners across the world (International Youth Foundation, 2007, in Bleckmann and Krüger, 2007, p 18).

Finally, the 'Asset-Based Community Development' approach (ABCD) has become a guideline for creating concrete resources for youth activism in a community-development context. For example, the 'Can-Do' toolkit 'Teens Action Packs' developed by Tony Gibson provides young people with tools for becoming involved in joint planning and action to rebuild marginalised communities, as described by Pike (2003). The approach shifts the focus of attention from problems and deficits to community assets, which include the individual capacities of local residents, their skills and talents and their motivation to contribute to positive changes in their communities (Scarman Trust, 2007, in Bleckmann and Krüger, 2007, p 17).

What emerged from this experience, and which YEPP builds on, were approaches that stressed the positive features of communities, such as the individual capacities of local residents, explicitly including young people and their associations, and their motivation to contribute to positive change in their communities; the power of local associations; the resources of public, private and non-profit institutions; and the physical as well as the economic resources of local communities and neighbourhoods (Scarman Trust, 2007, in Bleckmann and Krüger, 2007, p 22; Council of Europe and European Commission Youth Research Partnership, 2005, p 26). Thus a key conclusion of this work is the recognition that community development efforts must involve capacity building and, *ipso facto*, social-capital growth as fundamental strategies.

For YEPP it was important to build on the community development approach because, as Henderson and Vercseg (2010) put it:

> community development has become an activity that contributes to social integration and community cohesion. It is able to increase civil society's potential to take initiatives and action. It is able to help the transformation or re-establishment of society's institutional systems; it can bring together the various interests in society and build partnerships at both regional and society-wide levels. Finally, it can increase society's capacity for democratic self-organisation. (Henderson and Vercseg, 2010, p 32)

Community education

The other important influence on YEPP is the long-standing community education model, which is closely related to the community development approach. Both are based on the same philosophy and principles. Community education provides opportunities for the learning and capacity building of citizens, which is a key element of community development and contributes to the empowerment of a community as a whole (Krüger, 1997).

The community education model was first proposed by Dewey in the 19th century (Dewey, 1899). Since then there has been growing interest in implementing community education in many countries. In 2001, at the 'World Conference on Community Education' in Vancouver (Canada), community education practitioners agreed on the following understanding of community education:

> Community education is a concept whereby local citizens, schools, agencies, institutions and businesses become active partners in addressing education and community concerns.
>
> It is a community development process that utilizes the educational system as a catalyst for bringing community members together to identify and link community needs and resources in a manner that helps people to raise the quality of life in their communities.
>
> It is an educational philosophy that embraces these beliefs:
>
> • Education is a lifelong process;
> • Everyone in the community – individuals, businesses, public and private agencies – shares responsibility for the mission of educating all members of the community;
>
> Citizens have the right and a responsibility to be involved in determining community needs, identifying community resources and linking those needs and resources to improve their communities. (World Conference on Community Education, 2001)

In the professional debate about community education, the International Community Education Association has identified the following agreed key principles of community education:

Community education:

- aims to empower the individual and the community including educational, social, cultural, economic, legal, political dimensions;
- follows a holistic and community-based approach and comprehensive strategy;
- is needs-related, responding to individual and community needs;
- is learner- and community-relevant, addressing key issues of the individual and the community;
- promotes lifelong and life-wide learning which encompasses all aspects and all phases of life, promoting the vision of becoming an active participant of different learning communities throughout life;
- promotes participation/community involvement/ community action; generates and regenerates community and rebuilds social capital;
- promotes self-initiative/entrepreneurship/community business;
- brings about change by implementing interdisciplinary, multi-agency and trans-sectoral cooperation and partnership and by building sustainable networks;
- supports and is committed to community development and community renewal (Krüger and Zimmer, 2001).

Furthermore, community education seeks to facilitate the development of cognitive, creative and affective competencies, along with the personal confidence and the capacity to act in order to be the subject – not the object – in the management of all aspects of personal and community life, and to become an agent of change for the benefit of all, improving the quality of life.

Empowerment and partnership in YEPP

Empowerment

Empowerment is a widely discussed concept in an extensive international literature and, as a result, has a wide range of meanings with individual and social connotations that must be taken into account in a programme such as YEPP, which sets out to increase empowerment both for citizens and communities in different countries and also to measure change. For YEPP, youth empowerment 'is about young people gaining greater control over their individual and collective lives and destinies and having the ability to contribute effectively to the advancement of society. It is about opening up choices and facilitating better opportunities' (Krüger, 2002). Since youth empowerment is viewed as being embedded in community empowerment, it follows that changing the environment in which youth grow up will have a permanent impact on them.

Some of the key aspects mentioned in this brief definition are shared among many authors, such as Friedman (1992) and World Bank (2002). In John Friedman's understanding, empowerment refers to all those processes that lead people to take control and ownership of their lives, and requires, according to Nina Strandberg (2001), an array of opportunities to choose among. This understanding of empowerment overlaps with the concept of human development when defined as a process of enlarging people's choices. Strandberg (2001) further conceptualises empowerment as a 'transformative process' that is experienced both on the personal and the collective level (p 3).

There have been several attempts to identify levels of empowerment, but (despite the use of various terminologies) there are commonalities between different authors' views. Friedman (1992) suggests differentiating psychological empowerment, social empowerment and political empowerment. In a comparable way, Becker and Weyermann (2006) identify the individual level ('power within'), the level of the close social context ('power with') and the broader context of changing social power relations ('power over'). Developments on all three levels are, according to these definitions, interlinked and cannot be separated. On an individual level, empowerment includes the personal development associated with an increasing self-confidence and a deepening of the understanding of one's own situation.

This process of increasing personal awareness is often perceived as a crucial precondition for change, yet empowerment cannot be reduced to the individual level alone. The social and political levels are critical to exerting power and making real choices. The second level (social empowerment/power with) acknowledges the fact that 'change can take place when people work together. This involves thinking, acting and networking with others' (Becker and Weyermann, 2006) (in both conventional and new ways, such as through Facebook and Twitter). Ultimately, empowerment includes the macro-level as well, and must be concerned with changing realities and power relationships.

In their analysis of women's projects in developing countries, Rodenberg and Wichterich (1999) identify further aspects of empowerment. Similarly to the three levels mentioned above, they speak about 'personal empowerment', 'social empowerment', and 'political empowerment'. Additionally, they coined the terms 'cultural empowerment', 'legal empowerment' and 'economic empowerment'. By economic empowerment they are referring to economic literacy, property, social security and decision-making power regarding money. Legal empowerment includes legal security, knowledge of the existing laws and the ability to influence legislation. Cultural empowerment, finally, includes the power to shape cultural definitions and influence the symbolic order. In their view, empowerment processes can lead to changing social relationships and those socio-cultural norms which entail discrimination.

According to several authors, the concept of empowerment as such is also a critique of how the clients of social welfare programmes have been traditionally understood. These individuals and groups have typically been defined by their deficiencies rather than by their capacities, experiences and aspirations. As a consequence, willingly or unwillingly, there is an inherent power relationship between providers of assistance and their needy clients, who are dependent on assistance. The empowerment approach was developed to break up this power relationship by viewing disadvantaged groups as potential actors for change. It is driven by an inherent trust in people's strengths and on a normative orientation toward principles of autonomy, social justice and democratic participation (Bleckmann and Krüger, 2007, p 12). The International Youth Foundation emphasises the following elements of youth empowerment, which were taken up in the creation of YEPP in its concepts of youth and community empowerment:

- Competence – possessing the cognitive, social, emotional, vocational and civil skills needed for productive living;
- Confidence – having a sense of self-worth and an awareness of one's progress in life and projecting into the future;
- Character – having a strong sense of responsibility that guides their conduct, life decisions, and principles; and
- Connectedness – having a strong sense of security and belonging, and meaningful roles in the community. (International Youth Foundation, 2007, in Bleckmann and Krüger, 2007, p 12)

Partnerships

An important outcome of community development work and community education is recognition of the need to create strategic long-term, cross-sectoral partnerships to tackle problems on the ground. It is widely recognised that complex and deeply entrenched youth and community disempowerment and social exclusion in marginalised communities requires integrated and holistic approaches and systematic changes within the entire community, based on partnership across the sectors. Preferably, the partnerships should involve the public, private (for example, business) and independent sectors (for example, foundations, nongovernmental organisations (NGOs), civil society in general, religious groups). The importance of such partnerships has been recognised by the International Youth Foundation (2002) in the context of the Convention of the Rights of the Child (UN, 1990). The International Youth Foundation also notes that many positive outcomes for young people have been strongly influenced by the creation of cross-sectoral partnerships.

Cross-sectoral partnerships offer flexible opportunities for cooperation both locally and on the transnational level. An advantage of partnership building is that the different partners can contribute their specific strengths to the joint initiative:

> Governments offer the possibility of institutionalising and/ or scaling up activities to the national level. Businesses bring to the partnership financial assets, human intellectual capital, understanding of their industry, and in some cases, leverage or a power base. Civil society organisations offer the partnership a non-profit financial and programmatic infrastructure, development expertise and networks to reach beneficiaries. (Reese et al, 2002, p 41)

In most European countries, there is a tradition of cooperation and partnership of varying degrees and different qualitative levels between the public and the independent sectors in the field of youth and community development, while cooperation with the private sector in this field is a comparatively recent development. However, during the past few decades, many private companies have committed themselves to corporate social responsibility initiatives, a development which provides new opportunities for cross-sectoral partnerships. Business for Social Responsibility, an international organisation that helps member companies to achieve commercial success in ways that respect ethical values, people, communities and the environment, has found that:

> more companies than ever before are engaged in serious efforts to define and integrate corporate social responsibility into all aspects of their business, with their experiences being bolstered by a growing body of evidence that corporate social responsibility has a positive impact on business economic performance. (Business for Social Responsibility, 2007, in Bleckmann and Krüger, 2007, p 28)

This quote indicates that corporate social responsibility initiatives do not necessarily contradict economic goals – on the contrary, in many cases corporate social responsibility programmes have become a comparative competitive advantage. For instance, by investing in people and the environment, businesses also ensure their own commercial success, enhancement of their brand image and expansion into emerging markets. 'Given that one quarter of the world's total wealth is tied up in "brand value", appearing socially responsible is key, since brand value depends greatly on public perception' (Reese et al, 2002, p 9).

New trends show that community investment is gaining greater importance within corporate social responsibility. Companies interested in contributing to community development have a wide range of actions available to them. Typically, corporate community investment includes philanthropic cash and product donations to non-profit organisations, corporate incentives for employee giving and employee volunteer programmes. Many companies supplement monetary giving with service donations, technical support, skill donation and management advice designed to have a lasting benefit and impact for the communities as well as the company.

Corporate investment in communities has resulted from the growing societal expectation that corporations, 'as powerful societal players', should be contributing to improving the quality of life for residents, creating economic opportunities and sharing wealth and skills. The way companies approach their philanthropy has changed significantly over the years. Increasingly, companies see corporate social responsibility contributions as one component in a broad, comprehensive community investment strategy. Companies are increasingly forming long-term partnerships with non-profit organisations, built on the shared or complementary strengths of companies and their partners. A small but growing number of companies are viewing community investment as a way to help communities to become the drivers of their own development.

The YEPP 'empowerment matrix'

Empowerment and partnership are complex concepts that are central to YEPP. As a result an 'empowerment matrix' (Bleckmann et al, 2005, p 12) was constructed to clarify the meaning of these terms for YEPP, as shown in Table 1.1. It should be stressed that the components of the matrix are viewed as being mutually interdependent. The matrix was used by the Local Support Groups to help them reflect on aims and goals that might be identified and achieved.

Table 1.1: YEPP's empowerment matrix

Areas	Individual	Community
Personal-social	Identity Confidence and values Social skills Personal relationships	Community image and identity Social capital
Political	Active youth participation Skills and knowledge about participation	Self-organising ability of the population Participation opportunities Transparency of the public sector
Economic	Employability, entrepreneurship Skills and knowledge about the economy and working life	Working and training opportunities Economic development
Cultural	Cultural identity Values and attitudes Respect Intercultural knowledge and skills	Integration of various cultural groups Rich artistic/cultural life
Education and training	Motivation, capabilities Formal educational and training successes	Educational opportunities Quality of schools (general and vocational education)
Legal	Legal knowledge	Civil rights
Health and environment	Mental and physical health Knowledge about health Respect towards nature	Health services Unpolluted environment Public awareness of the environment

The matrix makes it clear that to empower young people and communities requires a multi-dimensional and multi-sectoral approach that is consonant with the complexity of the problems faced by them. As noted in the preface, worldwide experience in the field of youth and community programmes suggests that the limited impact of the traditional, piecemeal approach can only be overcome through:

- interdisciplinary and integrated approaches;
- pooling expertise, experiences and resources of the public, private and independent sectors;
- developing joint action and working in partnership across boundaries, based on shared values and goals;
- holistic community and needs-based approaches;
- influencing local public service structures, relevant legal regulations and policies in the field of youth and community development.

Non-negotiable key features of YEPP

Based on the thinking lying behind it, YEPP is, first and foremost, a programme to create change in communities. Derived from discussions of youth and community empowerment, YEPP developed 10 non-negotiable key features that have become part of the common ground of all YEPP stakeholder groups. They are:

1. **Starting from the needs of the local community and mobilising local resources**
   Locally owned and developed innovations must meet the local needs and actively involve local resources.
2. **Establishing cross-sectoral partnerships**
   Long-term and systemic change in communities can only be brought about through joining forces and coordinating the efforts of individuals, organisations and other stakeholders in the community.
3. **Involving local stakeholders in strategic planning, implementation and evaluation**
   The local stakeholders are encouraged and trained to participate actively in all parts of local programme development, thus creating change.
4. **Creating opportunities for young people's active participation in decision making**
   Supporting young people's empowerment requires that young people are viewed as competent individuals and potential agents of change. When youth are listened to and trusted, they expand their capabilities and are able to become more active and responsible citizens.

5. **Integrating action and reflection**
   The local development process is supported by regular, systematic evaluation and feedback.
6. **Bridging gaps between schools, youth, the community and informal education**
   Schools are needed as active contributors to positive community development and youth empowerment. This requires that schools open their doors to the community and cooperate constructively with it.
7. **Investing in (young) people's capacities**
   Long-term changes require capable people to pursue agreed-upon goals. Through capacity building in formal and non-formal settings, (young) people's ability to create changes in their community is strengthened.
8. **Providing equal opportunities**
   Equal opportunities and respect for young people of both genders and from all cultural and ethnic backgrounds are fundamental principles of YEPP.
9. **Integrating the local and the transnational areas of work**
   The local development processes are supported systematically by a transnational working and learning network, and the partners in YEPP jointly develop new transnational initiatives.
10. **Advocating for new policies**
    Policies targeted at youth at risk and the communities in which they live are often fragmented and deficit oriented. The partners of YEPP advocate more holistic approaches that follow principles of empowerment, participation and partnership.

TWO

YEPP I: implementation

The previous chapter outlined the broader context in which YEPP has been created and explained its key concepts of empowerment and partnerships. This chapter provides an account of the implementation of YEPP I, its concept of change and the method used to evaluate changes on the ground.

The YEPP Concept of Change in practice

YEPP was implemented in six European countries, in seven disadvantaged areas. These sites are known as 'Local Programme Sites'.[1] The countries and sites involved are:

- Belgium: Antwerp-North
- Bosnia and Herzegovina: Tuzla (Simin Han)
- Finland: Kristinestad
- Germany: Mannheim (Neckarstadt-West)
- Ireland: Dublin (North-East Inner City)
- Italy: Turin (Mirafiori South)
- Italy: Turin (Parella).

Local Programme Sites are both rural and urban areas where social and economic problems are at such a level that they are seriously detrimental to the general prospects of children and youth. In addition, Local Programme Sites already contain a large number of initiatives intended to engage with young people and the communities in which they live. However, despite these actions, which tend to be fragmented, there remains a need for further investment in order to provide more comprehensive joint strategies through the development of partnerships.

YEPP is both a national and an international project and the principles given in the previous chapter work at both of these levels. Thus, each national YEPP site functions independently within its own national and local context *and* at the transnational level, through which the actors involved in each of the Local Programme Sites meet regularly to support each other, share information, build capacity and plan new transnational projects and events.

YEPP was created by a group of foundations in the context of the EFC to develop a coherent response to youth and communities that were experiencing substantial difficulties and where foundations were already working at a high level of intensity. These foundations made up the main part of the steering committee of YEPP and provided the necessary funding. This committee worked under the auspices of NEF.[2]

A particular feature of YEPP was the involvement of Peter Evans of CERI at the OECD. As a member of the CERI secretariat, he became involved in YEPP through earlier work on integrating services for children and youth at risk that had been supported by one of the key foundations involved in establishing YEPP – the Charles Stewart Mott Foundation of the US. The main role of CERI in YEPP was to carry out an 'external evaluation', but the overall design of the evaluation of YEPP I was developed by the authors.

The steering committee appointed one of the developers of YEPP, Angelika Krüger, as the programme director, who was based at the International Academy in Berlin and who had the responsibility to appoint a small team to make YEPP work. This group, known as the Programme Team, supported and reported on the work in the Local Programme Sites through regular visits, technical advice, capacity building and so on. The programme team was also central in maintaining the dynamism of YEPP, supporting the transnational work, arranging annual conferences and, of course, reporting to the steering committee, NEF and the EFC.

As a result of this structure, individual foundations that were members of the steering committee, agreed to support the implementation of YEPP in sites in which they were already funding certain actions. This opened the way for the preparation of analyses of local needs and resources which formed the starting-point for the identification of goals to be achieved. During the preparation of these reports Local Support Groups were established and local coordinators and researchers, paid by the foundations at local level, were identified. The Local Support Groups were made up from key local actors from the three sectors – public, private and independent – and, crucially, they included representatives of local young people. The local coordinators and researchers were also members of the Local Support Groups.

The role of the Local Support Groups is to jointly develop holistic needs-based action plans (known as operational plans), to prioritise goals for the community to achieve, to plan the means to achieve them, to monitor and evaluate progress and, in the light of experience, to identify new goals and to continue with this cycle during the continuation of YEPP.

Thus the Local Support Groups were implementing an action research model as described, for example, by Kurt Lewin (Smith, 2001), where the linking of inputs to outcomes provides good evidence for causality, and which has been incorporated into YEPP's cycle-of-change model. This approach has remained consistent throughout YEPP I and II, and is represented in Figure 2.

Figure 2: YEPP's cycle of change at the local level

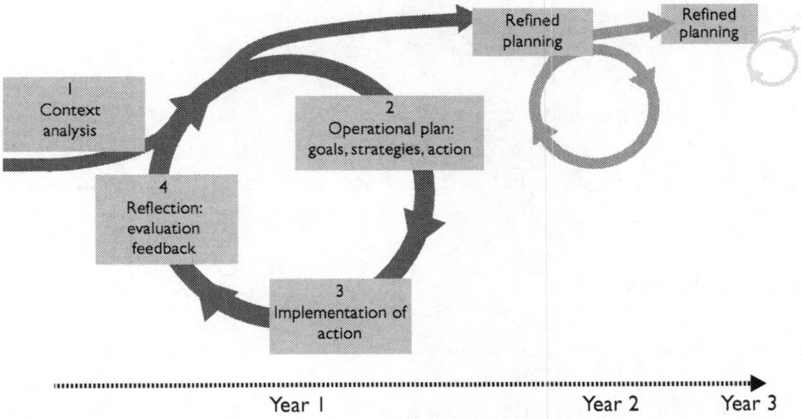

The evaluation design

YEPP I was a complex international action research project that involved individuals and institutions at different levels alongside an on-going evaluation of progress. The actors included policy makers in government departments, foundations and businesses, those working locally either as administrators or in the field and the clients. The inclusion of these different levels was based on earlier OECD work that identified the importance of including representatives of the mandating, strategic, operational and field levels in the analysis (OECD, 1998). It was agreed at the outset that the gathering of information from these sources, which would make up the database for the evaluation, would be shared between the programme team and the OECD/CERI. The former would be responsible for the 'internal evaluation' covering data gathered from field work, while the OECD/CERI would carry out the 'external evaluation' by focusing on actors at policy and transnational levels and would serve to confirm aspects of the internal evaluation. Both elements of the evaluation are based on Stufflebeam's CIPP model (Context, Input, Process, Product) (Stufflebeam, 1988), which should allow the final evaluation to bring the results of these two processes together. This process was facilitated by the use of N6 (NUD*IST) software (QSRinternational, 2002). The main results for each Local Programme Site are described in Chapter Three.

Thus, the general aims of the evaluation are to:

- monitor the process of the programme on all levels;
- provide regular feedback to the local and transnational levels of the programme;
- improve the implementation and the outcomes of local programmes and the transnational activities through analysing supporting factors as well as obstacles;
- disseminate experiences and lessons learnt;
- improve future programming of the participating foundations;
- influence local, national and international policy making through evidence-based recommendations and analysis.

The internal evaluation

The internal evaluation was under the responsibility of the Institute for Community Education of the International Academy for Innovative Pedagogy, Psychology and Economics (INA/ICE) at the Free University of Berlin, which developed, implemented and evaluated YEPP.

The internal evaluation was conceptualised to reflect the participatory action research model adopted by YEPP I and therefore had to involve the perspectives of the actors and participants in each Local Programme Site at operational and field levels. It was conducted by the programme team in collaboration with the local researcher in each site. The role of the local researcher was to be a 'critical friend' who would be able to move fluidly about the system, have access to all relevant materials, participate in meetings and communicate easily with key stakeholders.

The local researchers provided an initial background report on each site, the context analysis, and subsequent regular reports on progress using the empowerment matrix, to help them to reflect on relevant areas of change including information on cross-cutting themes, especially on youth and community empowerment and cross-sectoral partnerships. The YEPP Programme Team prepared reports on the transnational aspect of YEPP.[3] This information was summarised for each Local Programme Site, using the CIPP categories, in case studies by the programme team or, in some cases, by the local researcher, alongside information gathered by the programme team through regular visits to and communications with the sites.

At the end of YEPP, the programme team presented a cross-cutting analysis of the results of the internal evaluation (Bleckmann and Krüger, 2007).

The external evaluation

The external evaluation was conducted by the OECD/CERI. It had a simpler structure than that of the internal evaluation, comprising one visit to each site in 2004 and 2005. In total more than 330 individuals from the mandating and strategic levels, representing local, regional and national levels in the public, private and independent sectors, provided data, using semi-structured interviews that probed for information, using the CIPP categories, about youth empowerment, community development and partnerships. The individuals interviewed came from all levels, from policy makers to those closely associated with specific developments in the Local Programme Sites, and the information gathered was summarised in a report (OECD/CERI, 2007).

Notes

[1] In YEPP I these sites were referred to as 'Centres of High Intensity' (CHIs). This term was replaced in YEPP II by 'Local Programme Sites'. As a result, the term Local Programme Site(s) is used throughout this book.

[2] Originally this was the Association for Innovative Cooperation in Europe (AICE) that was renamed as NEF.

[3] All of these reports are based on data gathered systematically and consistently through individual and focus group interviews with key stakeholders, including young people, informal communication with stakeholders, participant observations in meetings, individual case studies of young people and structured discussions in the Local Support Groups. They are available from the YEPP International Resource Centre (IRC) at INA/ICE in Berlin.

THREE

YEPP I: key changes in YEPP Local Programme Sites

This chapter provides summaries of the key changes that took place in the YEPP Local Programme Sites based on data provided in both the internal and external evaluation reports. The first to be described are those sites where YEPP was well implemented: Tuzla-Simin Han in Bosnia and Herzegovina, Turin-Mirafiori in Italy and Kristinestad in Finland. Next are those where there was only partial implementation: Turin-Parella in Italy; Antwerp North in Belgium and Mannheim Neckarstadt-West in Germany. Dublin North East Inner City in Ireland is the last Local Programme Site to be presented, since it became part of YEPP much later in the development of the work. These summaries are all structured in the same way. The sections describing the method used to create change are divided into goals, means and results within the different action research-based cycles of change. They are presented in this way in order to highlight the links between intention (goals), the means used to create change and the results, and in order to emphasise the causal links.

As far as possible all of these skeletal reports are structured in the same way. They are based on much fuller reports covering some 600 pages.[1]

Well-implemented sites

Tuzla-Simin Han, Bosnia and Herzegovina

Background

Simin Han is a semi-rural district on the outskirts of the city of Tuzla in Bosnia and Herzegovina. Simin Han has been deeply affected by the war in the Balkans during the 1990s and by the move from communism to capitalism. After many demographic changes following the war, the population of Simin Han in 2006 was around 7,000–8,000, with a prewar-domiciled to post-war refugee ratio of about 1:2. This must be contrasted to a ratio of approximately 1:6 that obtained in 2002, nearer to the start of YEPP in Simin Han.

Economic recovery has been very slow, with little investment in recent years. This means that the unemployment rate is high, estimated to be between 50% and 70%. Furthermore, following the Dayton Peace Agreement after the war (Dayton Peace Agreement on Bosnia and Herzegovina, 1995), political organisation has changed, with many of the decision-making powers having moved from the municipal to the cantonal level.

As a result, on the one hand, there is a lack of social cohesion and community identity, and poor public and community infrastructure, while on the other hand, local participants are interested in long-term community and youth empowerment.

Precursors of YEPP

In 2001 Simin Han received considerable support from a number of NGOs, such as Prijateljice (a community women's organisation), the IPAK Youth Centre[2], the Parents' Association and the Students' Council. The Freudenberg Foundation was engaged in the long-term development of children and the community, and had a field office in Tuzla. Recently there has been more extensive involvement of the independent sector.

In addition, the only primary school in Simin Han, with pupils aged from 6–14 years, is at the centre of the district's renewal.

Motivation for YEPP

Tuzla is a city recovering from war, with many displacement problems and associated difficulties among the population. There has been a host of financial support from a wide range of government and non-governmental institutions. However, much of this was uncoordinated and there was a strong need for more holistic planning. In addition, because Bosnia and Herzegovina is in transition from a communist to a democratic society, there is a need to develop new attitudes and to involve young people in decision making and autonomous thinking.

YEPP's organisational structure

The Local Support Group comprised: Freudenberg Foundation; Ministry of Education, Science and Culture, Tuzla Canton; Ministry of Labour and Welfare Policy, Tuzla Canton; Primary School, Simin Han; Tuzla Municipality; Pupils' Council of the Primary School, Simin Han; Association of Parents; Local District of Simin Han; Prijateljice,

Simin Han; Youth Centre, IPAK; High School for Traffic Studies in Tuzla; Entrepreneurial Chamber of Tuzla and Tuzla Canton; Local Youth Council, Tuzla; German Organisation for Technical Cooperation (GTZ), Tuzla.

A local coordinator and researcher were appointed.

What changes did YEPP bring about in Tuzla-Simin Han?

Local actors, already interested in improving community cohesion, were brought together in the preparatory phases of YEPP to develop an action plan. Their involvement is reported as having been the key to the success of YEPP in Simin Han, since it gave ownership to the community. The action plan was presented to a number of other local participants, who came to form the Local Support Group. A year later (December 2002) a new operational plan was agreed – to be implemented by an executive group of the Local Support Group consisting of the Freudenberg Foundation local staff, YEPP volunteers[3] and two members of the Local Support Group.

First cycle: 2002–03
Goals:
- to empower young people through support in education and training, to provide employment opportunities, to develop self-initiative, self-organisational and entrepreneurial skills;
- to develop democracy and democratic culture, as well as to stimulate social cohesion through promotion of tolerance and the programme of civil society;
- to reconstruct the community and its infrastructure through the promotion of active citizenship and actions at the community level;
- to promote partnership among the three sectors: public, private and independent;
- to promote ecological issues and improve the environmental situation in the local community.

Means

Different segments of the local population over a wide age range were mobilised. These included citizens of Simin Han, internally displaced citizens and new inhabitants of Simin Han. Special attention was paid to gender issues, to issues of persons with special needs and to matters of social inclusion. The Charles Stewart Mott Foundation, Freudenberg Foundation and the local Soros Foundation agreed to cooperate so as to support YEPP in Simin Han.

- Employment and education: Professional orientation programme in the primary school; entrepreneurial youth training; 'The Point' (an agricultural cooperative); computer training for youth.
- Democracy: Youth Council; Pupils' Council.
- Community area of reconstruction and the action at community level: Reconstructing the former offices of the salt mines to become a community centre called the Agora.
- Establishing the Community Foundation – Simin Han, for future sustainability of YEPP.
- Ecology training and campaigning.

Results:

- Employment and education: Participation by 123 students in 2002, bringing together students, teachers, employers and the wider community to develop a dialogue on the issues.
- The Point: Coordinator selected, contacts made in public, private and independent sectors; a legal framework was developed and a home base was secured.
- The Agora: A 10-year lease of the offices of the salt mines was agreed with the district administration. The offices were refurbished, with opening of the Agora planned for September 2003.
- Community Foundation: Planning for the establishment of the Community Foundation was undertaken. Prijateljice played a large role in this and the community foundation was registered in July 2003. It was agreed that three young people under the age of 26 must be on the board. An action plan was developed.
- Ecology training: Thirty people from different groups trained as leaders of ecology projects and were supported by the Heinrich Böll Foundation in Sarajevo, in a joint project with the primary school, the Freudenberg Foundation and the Association for Education, Ecology and Economy Tuzla-3E.
- Councils of pupils and parents: These were one of the few such councils in the whole of Bosnia and Herzegovina. They influenced policy making and were instrumental in the passing of the law on primary education in the Tuzla canton.
- Networking and public presence: A regular information bulletin was established, together with good relations with local media.
- Transnational involvement: Visits to Berlin and Kristinestad took place and the Finnish team was received in Simin Han.
- Capacity building and institution building: a continuous effort was made to strengthen these areas via training, workshops and education.

Second cycle: September 2003–July 2004

The Local Support Group formally changed its name to the 'Advisory Board of the Community Foundation'. It met twice in this period.

The executive group of the Local Support Group was disbanded and replaced by the Local Actors' Roundtable, coordinated by the local coordinator. This group met monthly in the Agora.

Goals

These remained the same as for 2002–03.

Means:

* creation of the Youth Council;
* opening of the Agora with a donors' meeting;
* assignment of the community cafe;
* Community Foundation grants;
* two conferences on ecology;
* meeting of local coordinators from all the programme sites;
* foundation of a pupils' and a citizens' cooperative;
* training 'Business in Schools';
* peer leadership training.

Results

* New donors came on board.[4]
* The Agora: opened with a donors' meeting and other cultural activities. The cultural cafe opened.
* The Community Foundation agreed to use all its funds for the Youth Bank project; first grants were allocated and support was given to the campaign 'Safe Children in Traffic', organised by the Council of the local school and parents. The Community Foundation supported the transnational work within the framework of YEPP and joint international artistic projects, for example, the Antwerp workshop 'PARTicipation in the Picture'. An advertising campaign was planned and focus was placed on the importance of links with the private sector. The municipality of Tuzla contributed a giant chessboard outside the Agora and gave support to the 'Safe Children in Traffic' campaign.
* Youth Council: Established following the model seen in Kristinestad. The Youth Council engages in various projects, such as the Youth Bank, and takes part in the actors' round table and reaches out to youth in the Local Programme Site. It also developed links with other youth councils abroad.

- Business in schools: Two training sessions on entrepreneurship were held and cooperatives were opened in four schools. Simin Han primary school focused on honey production.
- The cooperative 'Kooperativa' was established to provide employment opportunities and also to involve more citizens in community development.
- The Point: Struggled to find the right role.
- Youth Bank: Ten students were involved in training.
- Vocational orientation: Seventh grade pupils with special needs were involved and given an opportunity to learn about various professions, including visits to offices and factories.
- Peer leadership training: Worked with the Swedish organisation Ungaomar; 12 youth were involved.
- Conferences on ecology: Activities were identified and groups were formed to implement them.
- Safe Children in Traffic: Various activities took place, one involving the police, to raise awareness of traffic and safety.

Third cycle: July 2004–December 2005
Goals
During this period the goals of YEPP Simin Han were revisited. In a first phase the intention was to consolidate the existing work and to introduce new topics, some of which would emerge from the original ones. A second phase would adapt these programmes and extend them into the whole of the city of Tuzla.

Means:
- community foundation receives new grants and expands;
- resource centre for open schools;
- cultural cafe in the Agora;
- leadership training;
- youth bank project;
- public campaigns (ecology and traffic);
- citizens' conference on the future of Simin Han;
- spring fair;
- summer youth camps;
- training for tourist guides;
- community arts project.

Results:
- Various new grants for the activities were received, some from new donors, for example, Pro Helvetia for the community arts programme. Some grants were also long term and help to sustain YEPP in Tuzla-Simin Han.

- The Community Foundation expanded from Simin Han to the canton of Tuzla. A partnership with the municipality of Tuzla was proposed.
- The Agora was refurbished, with help from youth leaders. A spring fair was held to promote YEPP and the Community Foundation and other initiatives. Also, regular cultural activities started.
- Simin Han primary school used 'activating'[5] interviews and hosted 'The Future of Citizens of Simin Han' conference. One hundred participants were involved in discussing their future and resolving problems.
- The Youth Bank, Youth Council and Leadership programme were viewed as a whole, rather than as separate activities. Regular meetings were held and activities were implemented.
- Open Centres and a Resource Centre for Open Centres were created in Simin Han in order to improve the functioning of the network of these centres, which are to encourage youth to take part in educational, social and economic processes.
- Business in school and the Kooperativa in Simin Han primary school continued to grow and to include professional honey producers, and offered training to other schools. However, the cooperative encountered legal problems and The Point project failed to take off.
- Tourist guide training was offered to 25 young people in Simin Han to become tour guides for Tuzla canton.
- Leadership training took place, some of it being international – for example, in Sweden, organised by Stiftelsen Konung Gustaf V.s 90-Arsfond. There was also training on the 'Can Do'[6] principles (Scarman Trust, 2007, in Bleckmann and Krüger, 2007). Other sponsors supported further training.
- New green group and EKO-Team focused on garbage removal and competitions, and also carried out training sessions and workshops.
- The vocational orientation programme expanded, involving more factories and other businesses, and opened students' minds to new possibilities.
- The Safe Children in Traffic activity developed petitions, for example, to set up new traffic lights and bus stops.

At the end of this period, YEPP Simin Han decided that, in order to achieve the goal of expanding the work into the city of Tuzla, the goals would have to be elaborated by the restructured Local Support Group of the local actors' roundtable and the advisory board. New operational plans would be prepared and the evaluation of the work would be streamlined into thematic areas. New strategic directions for the community foundation would be determined, focusing on policy-level impact and sustainability that would take into account the results so far obtained.

2006: New horizons

Although the Community Foundation Tuzla has taken over the implementation of YEPP from the Freudenberg Foundation, the latter still continues to support the work, and recommits itself to YEPP's aims and principles and sets about the task of revising its approach. In this process the results of the internal evaluation are used extensively to reshape the aims and objectives of the programme.

Comment

It is abundantly clear that YEPP Simin Han was a highly successful project in which the cycles of change were fully implemented. After a difficult start, during which the purposes of the research had to be learnt and understood, the work of the local researcher was very much appreciated and the research results were used to reflect on the experiences and to revise the programme.

Principal outcomes

Youth empowerment

The numbers of youths involved in this Local Programme Site grew immeasurably between 2002 and 2006. It must be remembered that these young people are vulnerable. They are living in a post-war environment and they are still very sensitive about the events that took place. Nevertheless, these young people gained new skills and knowledge and have grown in self-confidence and efficacy, in terms of their individual and collective engagement and actions both in Simin Han and more widely in the city of Tuzla. In other words, they have become empowered.

Community empowerment

The Agora provided a hub for the community to develop its social reality and also to improve its self-organisation skills to achieve political goals. New institutions have been created and citizens participate in decision making. In this, the Local Support Group and the Community Foundation were central in providing support and direction. Results in the economic area are less satisfactory. YEPP has not been successful in tackling the problems of unemployment, despite its best efforts.

Through its involvement with YEPP, the school is improving the quality of education in the Local Programme Site.

Partnerships

The independent sector

This sector has been hugely supportive of YEPP, and the various actors and groups have been very successful in involving new foundations and NGOs. Foundations have also cooperated with each other to achieve common goals.

The public sector

The public sector involvement has increased over time and the success of YEPP has allowed it to initiate actions, especially in the wider context of involvement in the city of Tuzla.

The private sector

As in the public sector, the involvement of the private sector has increased over the course of the YEPP work.

Trans-sectoral cooperation

The three sectors have also improved their collaboration over the period, although there has been a decrease in the quality of partnership between public and independent sectors, even though their collective ownership improved. Cooperation between the public and private sectors declined the most.

Transnational cooperation

Simin Han has been strongly involved in transnational cooperation by visiting the other Local Programme Sites, and also by hosting them. Links with other foundations have also been formed and exchanges made outside of the YEPP transnational arrangements. The workshops in Antwerp and Turin (PARTicipation and EmpowerMediaNetwork) have been especially empowering. Tuzla-Simin Han youth have, as a result, developed a very promising community TV project that has won a number of awards.

Sustainability

It is clear that sustainability has been on the minds of the YEPP team in Simin Han since the outset. The creation of first the Community Foundation and then the 'Community Foundation Tuzla' are excellent examples of the development of institutions to achieve sustainability. They have proved themselves by successfully taking over the management of YEPP Simin Han, and possibly creating YEPP Tuzla in the future.

Policy impact

The work in Simin Han and the creation of a community foundation has had a major impact. Before, community foundations were illegal in Bosnia and Herzegovina and the Community Foundation's creation would have been impossible without support from the public sector. The extension of this approach to the city of Tuzla as a whole is strong confirmation of its success and influence. Locally, the development of the Agora was carried out with full support from the public authorities and has been significant in developing democratic principles in the minds of the population.

Conclusions

It is quite evident that YEPP Simin Han has been a highly successful project and that the YEPP model of change was strongly implemented and fully appreciated by the participants. The feedback based on the evaluation proved extremely helpful for checking on progress and formulating new lines of action for the future, especially in the major evaluation and revision of the programme in 2006. It is also clear that YEPP has brought about many positive changes for both the community and its young people. Without the YEPP work these changes almost certainly would not have taken place.

Turin-Mirafiori, Italy

Background

Mirafiori Sud is a large urban area within the 10th local administration district on the outskirts of the city of Turin in north-west Italy. Shortly after the end of the Second World War, Mirafiori was a rural area, but it changed dramatically with the opening of the FIAT motor car factory. In less than 20 years the population grew from 3,000 to 40,000, with many families migrating from southern Italy. Although, in the beginning, the 'new' Mirafiori was a dormitory district with few services, there has been substantial investment and regeneration over the past 30 years, which has provided open spaces, schools, health services and improved transportation.

However, recent changes in the economy and the decline of FIAT in the 1990s led to high unemployment and increased poverty, and, although there is much local pride in the districts, Mirafiori as a whole is seeking a new identity. Mirafiori has a centre-left local council, its own budget and a mandate to 2011.

Mirafiori faces many challenges typical of such neighbourhoods:

- families with low levels of education and employment and other issues;
- high rates of drop-out and school failure;
- high rates of youth unemployment;
- street gangs.

Precursors of YEPP

A regeneration plan for Mirafiori was initiated in 1999 which included the improvement of council houses and other buildings, renewal of green areas and social regeneration, all with the active participation of the inhabitants. The plan was implemented by three social companies who worked with local residents, carried out conflict resolution between the actors, supported local entrepreneurship, supported the weakest elements of the local communities, promoted self-help networks and provided information on the on-going urban transformations. Each year the local district council outlines a youth plan and provides financial support for projects proposed by NGOs, associations and churches. The plan usually sustains activities that are very different from each other and are not interlinked.

Motivation for YEPP

Discussions between Compagnia di San Paolo and the city of Turin noted that YEPP's objectives and method were consistent with the city's new youth policies, which included the opening of meeting places, especially in those areas considered poor as far as social relations and opportunities for young people were concerned. The city wanted to give young people an opportunity to take an active part in the planning of these new meeting places – the so-called 'TO & TU' centres – and in creating local networks.

Mirafiori Sud, District 10 was identified by the city of Turin as a Local Programme Site, since there was a lack of local youth policies, resources and initiatives for local young people. In addition, a new youth centre was scheduled to be opening in the near future.

YEPP started its work in Mirafiori in late 2002 and built on the existing structures.

YEPP's organisational structure

YEPP Mirafiori appointed a local coordinator and researcher and created a Local Support Group. A youth forum was established that was involved in the development of the operational plans.

What changes did YEPP bring about in Mirafiori?

Between the spring of 2003 and the spring of 2006 the YEPP problem-solving model went through two full cycles and began on a third. The period between March and October 2003 was viewed as a settling-in phase. It took a full year between the first meeting of the YEPP local team with representatives of the Mirafiori Sud district to appoint a local coordinator and researcher, who would work together during the following three years and prepare the first operational plan. However, this period of time was not lost, and served to introduce YEPP to Mirafiori. A YEPP Youth Forum Meeting was established that met on a number of occasions. It identified the following issues to be addressed:

- the lack of meeting places for young people;
- the need for free time and job opportunities;
- capacity building in small social agencies;
- need to support youth at risk;
- overcoming the physical fragmentation of the area;
- overcoming the feeling of isolation from the city of Turin;
- the lack of youth policies;
- the fragmentation of youth policies and lack of networking opportunities between local actors;
- overcoming the negative perceptions of Mirafiori and its image as a 'bad place', since, according to local residents, this was no longer true.

There was agreement, although not unanimous, to begin the process by holding a festival at the end of September 2003. Although the event itself was successful, many tensions emerged among the organising group. There was no real cooperation among the members of this group, and from this point of view the festival was perceived as failing to meet the YEPP model.

It became clear that the working methods of the local coordinator were not compatible with those of YEPP, and she was replaced towards the end of 2003. In addition, the majority of young people involved, although coming from disadvantaged families, were educated to university level.

First cycle: autumn 2003 to autumn 2004

The previously established 'forum' was replaced by a Local Support Group, which wished to develop a sense of belonging and worked long hours to define the first operational plan, which was achieved on time in February 2004. In September 2004 a new start was made in the light of a review of the operational plan. Up to this point, cultural and social areas had been stressed, which led to some participants lacking a role. Based on a further consideration of the empowerment matrix, political and economic areas were identified as additional priorities for development in the following cycle.

Goals:
- film and video: training in film-making and shooting of films about Mirafiori;
- music: census of musicians and bands in Mirafiori, followed by a three-day musical event with prizes;
- communication: identifying a mixed group of key people representative of all of the groups of youngsters to be contacted and involved, and producing YEPP advertisements involving as many young residents as possible;
- web design and skill development: training youth in web content management (Tiki wiki) and supporting reading and writing skills through new media linked to traditional forms of learning (the so-called 'Digital Creature'[7]).

Means:
- establishment of sub-groups responsible for specific actions and plenary sessions;
- street educators to engage youth in film-making;
- meeting of both Turin Local Programme Sites[8] with members of the YEPP steering committee and training company METODI to work on community development;[9]
- on-going discussions with the city of Turin and the district council.

Results:

- Turin meeting of YEPP the steering committee, programme team and local coordinators confirmed the YEPP approach.
- Construction of a network among participating organisations via the YEPP working method of participatory planning, which led to the formation of a project management model with a vision of the future.
- Appreciation of the importance of the sharing of individual and organisational knowledge, essential for the development of good work.
- YEPP addressed all youth in Mirafiori Sud, not only those at risk. This was a major policy change.
- After much negotiation between YEPP and the district's representatives, the joint management of the youth centre was given to members of the YEPP support group, although not to YEPP itself.
- Production of a short film by late spring 2004, involving street children and Roma.
- A second film was made in the autumn.
- Advertisements about YEPP were made.

Second cycle: winter 2005 to winter 2006

Work began with a one-day retreat in the hills of Piedmont, which proved to be an important stage and turning-point in the MiraYEPP[10] development. Based on YEPP's empowerment matrix, project areas for further development were identified, as were quality criteria for all future MiraYEPP activities. These were:

- network: plan and implement any activities in groups of at least three organisations;
- environment: consider environmental sustainability in all projects;
- areas: involve several districts – ideally all of them;
- young planners: at least one young person from the community participates in the planning stage and/or leads the activities;
- gender: attention to the female part of the youth population;
- competence handover: projects must generate a handover to youth and to the network of typical skills of the third sector (organisation, fund-raising and so on);
- durability: durable projects, not just events, would be sought;
- international: transnational/intercultural aspects would, as far as possible, be included in each project (this was a non-binding criterion).

Goals:

- training opportunities
- entrepreneurship
- working opportunities

- active participation
- self-organising abilities
- active citizenship
- inclusion of disadvantaged young people
- transnational experiences.

Means:

- communication and politics/community media
- economics/incubator politics
- education/self-organisation
- non-formal learning.

Results

Community media:

- EmpowerMediaNetwork established: the first step to community TV in YEPP;
- international training course on community TV in Turin and collaboration with the private sector;
- Mirafuori TV was launched and an editorial office opened;
- movies made and presented at a public viewing to a wide range of community members;
- Mirafuori TV productions shown regularly on local TV channel.

Economic development – incubator of new enterprises:

- an incubator tailored for Mirafiori was developed, with assistance from a public-private training group;
- eight enterprises were incubated, involving a wide range of youth;
- three projects continued – two with some success.

Self-organising:

- school newspaper produced in high school;
- transnational;
- collaboration with Mannheim Neckarstadt-West and Kristinestad on economic incubator. Grant applied for from EC (but failed).

Public and independent sector collaboration

- Formal agreement signed between Compagnia di San Paolo and city of Turin Youth Departments and Districts. There were significant discussions but the outcomes were not implemented.

Third cycle: 2006–07

There was continuity between the actions of the second and third cycles. The Local Support Group expanded to include the Reginald Theatre Group and decided to continue working in the same four general areas of action that emerged during the second cycle based on the identified goals, namely:

- community media
- economic incubator
- self-organisation
- transnational experiences.

Means:

- New organisational structure for the editorial office of community TV;
- MiraYEPP community TV gets permanent office in Turin;
- Training given to group for matters related to social enterprise;
- Theatre involved as useful means to involve youth (especially females);
- Youth centre linked to 'radio pilot' – there will be technical training for programme production also linked to self-organising action at the local high school;
- Community Foundation established to fund the local project in the future;
- As part of learning about community foundations, the importance of 'door openers' in providing access to the public and private sectors was recognised and the approach was prioritised in 2006.

Results:

No results are available, since they fell outside the research reporting period of 2001–06. For further information, see Chapter 6, Turin-Mirafiori.

Comment

This overview of progress made by YEPP in Mirafiori provides enough evidence to confirm the view that YEPP did indeed 'cause' the changes observed during the three cycles. The failure of the festival activity during the settling-in phase to create the necessary partnerships – which emerged so strongly later – reinforces this conclusion. In other words, without YEPP, the changes would not have occurred.

Certainly, the desire to continue working together and to create a community foundation almost certainly would not have happened without YEPP.

It is important to stress the strong role that Compagnia di San Paolo played as a foundation throughout this whole process, and its willingness to support and fund the work because of its belief in YEPP. That Compagnia di San Paolo was a key player cannot be overlooked. Thus, it is possible that a variety of community development models would have had the same results with continued and reliable funding, and it may be this factor, and the planned international nature of YEPP, which so motivated the youth, that are the key issues. However, none of this is likely to have happened had not the core of YEPP been so successful in engaging the stakeholders on the Local Support Group. In this regard it is also important not to forget the roles played by the local coordinator and researcher, who were committed to YEPP and created a well-implemented model.

Principal outcomes

Youth empowerment

The youth addressed by MiraYEPP were those whose parents came from a low socioeconomic level. It is notable that at the outset many of these students were well educated, to university degree level. Those with more severe disadvantages were supported by social workers' organisations that were part of the Local Support Group. In addition, Arcobaleno supported mentally ill youth, with the aim of integrating them into mainstream life. It did not want to provide separate solutions. MiraYEPP became a single project with 'different doors' or points of entry for youth with different interests and approaches. This understanding continued throughout the project and was confirmed at the last evaluation meeting, in May 2006.

- In 2003–04, young people were involved in the project at all levels. They were all university-level students but they had left by autumn 2004, mainly because their interests became different from the new developments in the Local Support Group.
- Involvement of disadvantaged youth proved difficult, partly because it was difficult to achieve the right level of actions to engage the interests and abilities of these youth.
- There was no interest in participation in local political decision making.

Gender

At the beginning, MiraYEPP mainly involved boys. Efforts to include girls were given a high priority in the 2005 action plan, and were successful. Girls were included and active, and argued for women's employment opportunities at various levels.

Economic empowerment

The MiraYEPP incubator addressed issues of entrepreneurship and the needs of youth seeking help to access the labour market. In 2006 the Local Support Group was satisfied with the results.

Community empowerment

- At the outset there was a policy to involve community organisations. As a result these organisations were very heavily involved. YEPP created a new method of working for them, and this led to a strong network. The action research method and the on-going evaluation were central to these changes.
- The image of the community received a boost from Mirafuori TV and the enterprise incubator, thus it was seen as a place where interesting things happen and with potential for new enterprises.
- The Local Support Group acquired new skills.
- Continuity was assured by the creation of the Community Foundation.

Partnerships

The independent sector

Compagnia di San Paolo played a major role in YEPP, on the steering committee of the whole programme, and played an active part in the Local Support Group. It responded to funding requests, enabling the action plans to be implemented, especially in terms of knowledge and skill building, for example, in supporting the community TV. In addition, Compagnia was instrumental in helping to create the Community Foundation once it realised that MiraYEPP was serious about continuing the work. This approach was consistent with its transparent strategy of phasing out its funding. Nevertheless, it provided the first endowment to the Community Foundation.

Local associations and NGOs

The publicly funded local organisations that joined YEPP became the force for change and were responsible for all the planning, implementation and evaluation. And the more they networked and became involved in YEPP, the more autonomous and independent they became of the city's youth policies and the more they aimed to change the way social policies in Mirafiori were supported and implemented by the public authorities. The moral support of Compagnia was fundamental to their involvement and the development of the Community Foundation was the vehicle for supporting further reforms.

The public sector

Schools: Links with the local high school were limited because of different perceptions of the role of youth involvement in MiraYEPP. However, there was some improvement following the appointment of a new school principal.

Social services: Social services operate within a passive 'medical' model, in contrast to YEPP, which works through an empowerment process. Social services also funded some of the local associations that were members of YEPP. Because of these factors, and social services' broader remit, they did not become represented in the Local Support Group. However, good relations and communications were always maintained and the social services' representatives were interested in the progress of YEPP.

Public libraries: One library was a recognised meeting point for the community and was viewed as a 'community library'. The director was a lively partner at the beginning of YEPP but left the Local Support Group after one year. However, she continued to support YEPP and made the library available for YEPP activities.

District: The politicians and officers at the district level remained external and cautious observers at the Local Support Group. The agreement signed between the Compagnia di San Paolo and the city had no immediate impact but did serve to establish a useful and helpful relationship between the district and the local coordinator. This led to YEPP becoming accepted by the district as a local actor thereby, replacing the individual associations and being invited to organise activities under the auspices of YEPP.

The private sector

The private sector was not greatly involved, despite attempts to involve it at the outset. Later a public-private organisation participated in the incubator project and became a member of the Local Support Group, resulting in a member of this organisation joining the group in his own right with his own enterprise.

Trans-sectoral cooperation

Local Support Group members reached a high level of cooperation and eventually felt that they *were* YEPP. Meetings were enjoyable and not too 'official'. The Mirafiori experience was characterised by a balance of self-interest and idealism, and this helped to make it work. Nevertheless, collaboration with other sectors in the Local Support Group was non-existent, with the result that the group ended up as a network of independent associations.

Transnational cooperation

* Strong cooperation of the local coordinator and researcher with the programme team was a feature of the working method and benefited the development of MiraYEPP.
* Transnational experiences for the Local Support Group and youth emerged slowly and were transformed by the EmpowerMediaNetwork.
* The sense of MiraYEPP's belonging to the international YEPP developed slowly, but was cemented by the 2nd YEPP community conference, which took place in Turin in March 2006.
* Transnational work was very attractive to the youth and the youth meetings were empowering for them, giving them a sense of independence.

Sustainability

A Community Foundation was established to sustain the work.

Policy impact

Despite the agreement between the Compagnia di San Paolo and the city of Turin and the district, the impact of YEPP on local youth policy making was judged minimal, even though this was given a high priority by YEPP. By 2006 the district had taken no clear position on YEPP (perhaps because of the legal frameworks in operation). However, there were always good relations and the appointment of a new city councillor with interest in this area may change the situation in the future. Apart from the considerable local achievements there was modest success at the policy level. The signing of the agreement between Compagnia and the city of Turin Youth Department and Districts IV (Parella) and X (Mirafiori) is unlikely to have happened without YEPP, and the Youth Department's final acceptance by YEPP as a single entity was also a significant result. Furthermore, the city was involved in the Community Foundation and its establishment in 2006.

Conclusions

The YEPP model was well implemented in Mirafiori. It is clear from the description given above that there is good evidence that the YEPP process led to lasting change. The list of outcomes shows that both the community and the youth were more empowered and that strong and lasting relationships were developed in the Local Support Group. Fuller relationships between the independent sector and the public and private sectors were only just beginning to emerge. The transnational outcomes were especially valued and the creation of a Community Foundation to sustain the work is clearly linked to YEPP goals.

Kristinestad, Finland

Background

Kristinestad is a municipality comprising 10 villages located on the north-western coast of Finland in the region of Ostrobothnia. It is about 100 kilometres south of Vaasa. It is a rural area with a high proportion of Swedish speakers (57.6%, in comparison to the rest of Finland's 5.5%). Over the past 30 years there has been an increasing exodus from the region, with the result that there is a declining and ageing population. The primary production sector is in decline and most jobs are in the service sector. The municipality is safe, but there are limited opportunities both in the labour market and for recreation. These are the main challenges faced by the community.

Precursors of YEPP

In 1999, the municipality launched 'Expedition Kristinestad', as part of the EU Leader II programme, in order to encourage young people to take part in political decision making. 'Future workshops' took place on how to create a better Kristinestad. These workshops included Swedish and Finnish speakers and led to the creation of the Youth Council to promote youth participation in decision making.

This, in its turn, led to a programme called 'By-Pass' funded by the Foundation of Swedish Culture in Finland, which set out to achieve broad participation in the 10 villages that make up Kristinestad. It allowed for the creation of workshops to carry out situational analyses and develop ideas for the future.

YEPP Kristinestad built on these programmes and developed the Culture Café, the Youth Council and LUMA (the village music school), based on the Nordic community school principle and included in the YEPP operational plan.

Motivation for YEPP

Kristinestad is a rural community experiencing a declining population, especially of young people, who are leaving for the cities to find work. The need for YEPP was to find a means of reinvigorating the community so as to keep the young people by creating opportunities for them and enhancing their involvement in the community.

The structure of YEPP in Kristinestad

From the outset, a local coordinator and a local researcher were appointed. In addition there was a Local Support Group that, from the beginning, included three young people from the Youth Council.

Did YEPP cause change in Kristinestad?

In Kristinestad, between the winter of 2001 and December 2005, YEPP's action research model went through two full cycles and began on a third. Throughout this period the Local Support Group remained faithful to the fundamentals of its first needs assessment, as identified in the following list of the characteristics of the area:

- on-going emigration of young people;
- economic transition from primary production to industrial service sectors;
- limited educational opportunities in academic/polytechnic education;
- unemployment of young people;
- cuts in public services, including youth services;
- drug and alcohol abuse by young people;
- a decentralised school network, facing risks as a result of decreasing numbers of pupils;
- a long-standing network of traditional youth associations that is challenged by the need to maintain participation in voluntary work.

First cycle: winter 2001 to summer 2002

In implementing the first cycle three *goals* were set, with three *means* of achieving them; and three *results* can be described.

Goals:

- further integration into the health and welfare system;
- mobilisation of opportunities for young people;
- promotion of entrepreneurship.

Means:

- development of cultural meeting places to bring together Finnish- and Swedish-speaking Finns (extension of the Cultural Café);
- extension of the activities of the community school and the village music school (LUMA);
- promotion of a new project to encourage entrepreneurship, through surveys and study visits, leading to new proposals.

Results:

- January 2002: the Culture Café was further developed;
- February:
  - health and lifestyle project was proposed;
  - village music community school project (LUMA) continued;
- The entrepreneurship project did not happen, but in May the local coordinator and some young people attended the Berlin workshop entitled 'Entrepreneurship and Local Development Put into Practice – Workshop on Business Models'.

Second cycle: August 2002 to December 2003

In the implementation of the second cycle, the political impetus was increased. The goals remained the same but new *means* were identified and new *results* were obtained.

Means:

- YEPP was publicly launched;
- a manifesto on youth empowerment was developed;
- closer contacts were planned with the local council;
- closer contacts were planned with the Youth Council.

Results:

- Youth Council gained in relevance to youth projects;
- education, entrepreneurship and community school workshop;

- health and lifestyle project started, with funding;
- transnational links made with other Local Programme Sites;
- continuation of Culture Café;
- continuation of newspaper;
- discontinuation of LUMA;
- youth empowerment manifesto adopted by municipal council.

Other significant developments

In between the second and third cycles, a number of management and funding challenges emerged which certainly had the effect of slowing developments. Nevertheless, there was progress and new funding on rural development was secured from the EC.

During the spring 2004 the earlier Local Support Group initiative to strengthen schools' councils led to the development of a 'Little Parliament'[11] supported by the Youth Council, the Youth Office and the Local Support Group. It was also funded in part by the municipal board, leading to new projects being supported.

Third cycle: August 2005 to December 2005

In the implementation of the third cycle, although the Local Support Group was happy with the progress made, only *goals* and *means* were identified,[12] the latter by the Youth Council.

Goals:
- more emphasis given to youth empowerment.

Means:
- participation, influence and active citizenship;
- economy and workplace;
- public relations and marketing of the region;
- public transport;
- meeting places;
- cooperation and exchange across language barriers.

Comment

This outline of progress made by YEPP in Kristinestad provides enough evidence that YEPP did indeed cause change. In the first cycle, it is very likely that YEPP led to the development of the operational plan.

But, given that several of the projects were continuations of existing programmes, these extensions could well have happened without YEPP: for instance, if a foundation had simply provided funds to support development with no external support.

However, entrepreneurship, the one original innovation in the first cycle, did not take place, except to the extent that a group from the municipality attended the workshop in Berlin. This was most unlikely to have happened without YEPP.

In the second cycle, while the needs analysis remained the same, the scope of the work changed, especially in involving the public sector more fully through the local council and the Youth Council. Following the earlier meeting in Berlin, progress was made on the entrepreneurship project and transnational links were developed with other Local Programme Sites.

The increased planned cooperation and the development of the lifestyle and entrepreneur projects are clear candidates to be outcomes caused by involvement with YEPP, as also are the links with other Local Programme Sites, which are highly unlikely to have emerged without the YEPP transnational programme and the involvement of the programme team.

In addition, the confidence gained by the Local Support Group in determining a new vision is indicative of growing community empowerment, and perhaps helped it to overcome substantial obstacles and to continue its work in early 2004, albeit in a reduced way. Clearly, the difficulties that emerged in 2004 help in understanding and perhaps explaining the slowing of momentum that required external support from the programme team in order to help the Local Support Group refocus and initiate the third cycle. Nevertheless, these facts alone provide strong support for the view that YEPP had become a central part of the community-change process in Kristinestad.

The next section will focus on the main outcomes of the work during this period as they relate to empowerment, partnership and transnational and sustainability issues.

Principal outcomes

Empowerment

Youth empowerment

- Active citizenship and participation were encouraged via the introduction of ideas boards in schools and pupils' councils.

- Youth Council joined the Local Support Group and became involved in municipal decision making and providing opportunities for the involvement of young refugees.
- Involvement with this process changed the lives of the young people who took part via, for instance, engagement in local politics, increasing their confidence through involvement in transnational projects and enhancement of their communication skills.
- Opportunities were created for learning and capacity building, for example, an entrepreneurial skills project and social and cultural development.

Community empowerment

The Local Support Group was established and expanded as the work unfolded, and continued after the formal ending of the project and the withdrawal of funding. The Local Support Group had a strong influence on municipal decision making.

- The cultural café continued to encourage intercultural development.
- The local bi-lingual newspaper continues.
- The Little Parliament was established, derived from school-based pupils' councils. It has power to allocate funds for youth project proposals.
- Youth Council became the official vehicle for representations to the municipal council;
- Proposals were made to encourage more links with Finnish-speaking schools and with vocational education and training, and for a more practical education.
- A TV channel for youth was set up in secondary schools and had an impact on the school curriculum.

Partnership

The public sector

- The Municipal Board accepted the YEPP vision in its Budget and Economy Plan and agreed to consult the Youth Council on all relevant matters and to provide some funds for specific youth-led projects. However, in the event, it was not easy for the Youth Council to bring about sustainable change.
- The local council's Youth Office accepted YEPP as a strategic partner and recognised that new funding has helped to stimulate change.

- One of the Kristinestad village councils joined YEPP on the Music and Citizenship project.
- A wider link with the region of Ostrobothnia has been established in order to extend youth empowerment ideas.
- Kristinestad was involved in a national conference on youth empowerment.
- A visit from a South Korean delegation was made possible because of contacts made via the OECD.
- A Nordic Network was established.

The private sector

A link was established with a TV production company in Norway.

Transnational

Transnational activity included:

- visits to Local Programme Sites in other countries;
- an international youth workshop on music and citizenship;
- a bilateral visit to Tuzla, Bosnia and Herzegovina;
- education and entrepreneurship with the programme team;
- visits to Mannheim Neckarstadt-West and Turin;
- a community TV meeting in Italy;
- creation of links with Norway;
- attendance at YEPP All Community conferences;
- a visit by the National Youth Commission of South Korea;
- transnational work was seen as most important by youth;
- capacity-building opportunities through transnational activities.

Sustainability post-2005

Even though there were difficulties with funding and there was neither a local coordinator nor a local researcher until 2006, the work continued with:

- a conference on 'Education, Democracy and Influence';
- the newspaper;
- the EmpowerMediaNetwork;
- the Youth Council being given a bigger role;
- more engagement of the municipal council;
- strengthening of the Little Parliament.

Policy impact

YEPP in Kristinestad has had a considerable impact on local policies, with the Municipal Board incorporating YEPP's vision into its Budget and Economy Plan by consulting the Youth Council and agreeing to fund relevant projects. In addition, the local council's Youth Office accepted YEPP as a strategic partner and welcomed the impact that YEPP's additional funding was able to make.

Conclusions

The YEPP model was well implemented in Kristinestad. It is clear from the description given above that there is good evidence that the YEPP process led to the observed changes in this municipality. The list of outcomes shows that both the community and that youth were more empowered and that strong and lasting relationships were developed between YEPP, in the form of the Local Support Group, and the public sector. Some small progress was made with the private sector. The transnational outcomes were especially valued and the sustainability plans are clearly linked to YEPP goals.

The work in Kristinestad survived a difficult period during the implementation of YEPP, due to the withdrawal of the supporting foundation, on the basis of its policy of funding projects for a maximum of four years. However, YEPP Kristinestad survived, and that too attests to the strength of YEPP in this community.

Partly implemented sites

Turin–Parella, Italy

Background

Parella is a densely populated urban area within the 4th local administrative district on the boundary of the city of Turin in north-west Italy. The urban expansion of the area began between the two world wars, with much new development in the 1970s and 1980s, with the result that, in December 2006, Parella had a population of 48,236 inhabitants. The local council has a centre-left disposition.

Parella is a young, middle-class district, with just under 20% of its population under the age of 24. However, it does not have a strong identity based on shared significant local events. There are unrecognised pockets of disadvantage and economic and cultural poverty, and family difficulties are increasingly being recognised by teachers and social workers.

Precursors of YEPP

Until 2002, Parella had city-level policies aimed at the prevention of disadvantage, whereby the local administrative districts funded various independent sector projects – for example, churches, NGOs working with disadvantaged youth – but there were no locally coordinated projects. This changed when the newly elected district council started to increase its involvement in youth policy in 2002, and in 2004 youth policy was listed as a priority to be addressed. The district council began to involve various youth-oriented agencies, associations and cooperatives that were already working in Parella, in order to create a new youth policy framework. In line with municipal strategies, a Youth centre, in the development of which youth were to take the lead, was opened in 2006. It was expected that this centre would become the vehicle for change and new youth policy in Parella.

Motivation for YEPP

Discussions between Compagnia di San Paolo and the city of Turin noted that YEPP's objectives and method were consistent with the city's new youth policies, which included the opening of meeting places, especially in those areas considered poor as far as social relations and opportunities for young people were concerned. The city wanted to give young people an opportunity to take an active part in the planning of these new meeting places – the so-called 'TO & TU' centres – and in creating local networks.

Parella's District 4 was identified by the city of Turin as a Local Programme Site, since there was a lack of local youth policies, resources and initiatives for local young people. In addition, a new youth centre was scheduled to be opened in the near future.

YEPP started its work in Parella in 2002. The approach and goals of the policy environment were consistent with those of YEPP.

Structure of YEPP

YEPP-Parella appointed a local coordinator and researcher. In addition there was a Local Support Group, initially consisting of representatives of the following groups: District 4 Culture Department, Parella Social Services, Dante Alighieri lower secondary school and Italo Calvino primary school, Sole Luna Association, Mondo Erre Cooperative, Communita and Quartoere Cooperative, Rock e i suoi fratelli Association, La Paranza del Greco Association, Agnesci Torino 3, and Time Sport Association. In addition, there were representatives of two neighbourhood shopkeepers' associations, but they withdrew after three months, due to poor health. Later, Tecnologia Filosofica theatre joined, and also students from the high school.

What changes did YEPP bring about in Parella?

A central working group was established comprising a representative of the supporting foundation, the Local Programme Site coordinators for Mirafiori and Parella and the local researcher. This group met almost weekly during the first year – November 2002 to December 2003.

A meeting with the president of the local council confirmed YEPP's model as being consistent with his view of youth policy, and a letter was sent to local members of the youth development community to invite them to a meeting to discuss the YEPP approach. However, there was immediate resistance from Social Services, which ran most of the youth projects in Parella, and there was the additional concern that YEPP might duplicate the already existing Coordinating Committee of the Education Agencies – a round table aimed at exchanging information between the public and private agencies working with youth. An invitation to YEPP to join this committee was rejected by the local coordinator, on the grounds that YEPP needed autonomy – a decision that created immediate tensions.

Following a meeting in response to the president's invitation, a Local Support Group was established and met in February 2003. The group identified loneliness and isolation, especially outside school hours, as the main characteristic of young people's lives in Parella, and the lack of meeting places hardly helped. As a result, the group agreed to meet every 15 days or so to tackle this problem that it had identified.

The Local Support Group focused on the use of communication tools, especially a newspaper and video, as the main areas for action, and defined the target group as children and youth aged from 6 to 13. Efforts were made to work with the local high school, but these were not very successful.

First cycle: autumn 2003–summer 2004

After nine months of intensive discussions the first operational plan was formed with four main goals:

Goals:
- to create a community newspaper, *Quattro fogli in Parella*;
- to set up a folk-dancing workshop;
- to instigate local 'animations';
- to hold street parties.

Means:
- establishment of an editorial office with lower secondary school children; articles to be written by primary and lower secondary children and to include neighbourhood interviews;
- folk dancing lessons with primary school classes;
- children to involve parents and friends in dancing, on leaving school in the afternoons; the Local Support Group to hand out information on YEPP.;
- five open air parties; five-a-side soccer and volleyball, games, folk-dancing, concerts, theatre; gathering suggestions from young people and adults and promoting YEPP through, for example, T-shirts and headscarves sporting the YEPP logo.

Results:
- Newspaper: An editorial office formed and articles were written by children in two schools, on the computers. Interviews were carried out, organised by one association 'Sole Luna', which complained at a Local Support Group meeting that it was not being supported by others.
- Folk-dancing workshop: There was much enthusiasm for this, and parents and the schools agreed to fund extra meetings. After-school performance was welcomed.
- Street parties: Five parties took place, with mixed success.

Second cycle: September 2004–July 2005

Work began with the collection of proposals for a new operational plan. However, there were many overt tensions, especially between the local coordinator and the Local Support Group, which also seemed to lack enthusiasm. In order to move forward, the Local Support Group divided itself into sub-groups. There were also changes in its composition. However, following a meeting with the foundation, a new understanding about YEPP emerged and this led to discussions about a new organisational structure for the Local Support Group. The new operational plan was finally agreed in February 2005.

Goals:

- include young people in decision-making processes;
- encourage the acquisition of skills by youth;
- work to develop the local community;
- encourage intra- and inter-generational exchange and communication;
- enhance the social function of the schools;
- strengthen the network of relationships at the school and international levels;
- work towards financial autonomy and future sustainability.

Means

In Cantiere Cattaneo Parella Secondary School:

- three days dedicated to students, involving practical demonstrations of YEPP activities in workshops;
- weekly workshops on theatre, percussion, electronic music, juggling;
- application of the 'Can Do' method to actively involve students in organising one of the school's conferences;
- workshop on community TV.

In Cantiere Parella:

- involvement of pre-teens and teenagers and the scout group in linking with groups in the area, sports and circus arts;
- school workshops on traditional dancing, juggling, videos and theatre;
- further development of the newspaper;
- training for the planning and organisation of initiatives for youth with Officina Pulcinella (a local circus and arts group). This action became known as 'Project No Project'.

Results

- The workshops in Cantiere Cattaneo Parella Secondary School were not successful and had little impact.
- The youth thought that some of the objectives were unrealistic – a different strategy was needed for working with the school.
- Some youth benefited from the new experiences offered, for example, preparing a project proposal for the Italian Ministry for Work and Social Policies, supported by the Stranidea Cooperative (a new member of the Local Support Group).
- Workshops in Cantiere Parella were very popular but were not seen as being strongly linked with YEPP.
- Involvement in the newspaper was very patchy and did not achieve the goal of establishing links in the community. Some lower secondary school children did start to take the initiative and write articles from home rather than in school time.

For the Local Support Group
- There was substantial conflict in the Local Support Group over the division of funds for the agreed operational plan. There was learning about the functioning and difficulties of working in the Local Support Group.
- A new discussion on YEPP in the post-2005 period was begun.

Third cycle: September 2005–July 2006

Analysis of successes and failures of the second cycle was carried out with a focus on the future, based on YEPP's youth empowerment matrix. It was agreed that actions would concentrate on social, cultural and political themes, with emphasis being given to the first two. There were also discussions about finding a YEPP home/office that would give it a stronger sense of identity and existence. In early 2006, the Local Support Group met with the district's president and noted the relative lack of success of YEPP-Parella.

However, a new operational plan for 2006–07 was drawn up. It was divided into two parts, dealing with internal and external objectives separately.

Internal objectives:
- create connections and coordination between the plan's actions and among the member organisations;
- increase the visibility of YEPP;
- focus on competence building for YEPP participants;
- support and enhance the former Cattaneo Group, now renamed the 'Youth Group';
- involve the Youth Group members as peer leaders;
- cooperate with public and independent sectors.

External objectives:
- facilitate communication with youth groups and between youth and adults;
- increase opportunities for youth choice;
- help youth to acquire new competences;
- support the development of youth interests, autonomy and self-determination.

Means:
- multi-generational activities – for example, sports, family activities – to take place in the school gym and the youth centre;
- theatre;
- community TV;

> • creativity with discarded materials – initiated by Project No Project;
> • the newspaper.
>
> **Results:**
> • The newspaper was still in existence, with the next edition planned for 2007.
> • The work with children and families had taken place.

Comment

The Local Support Group in Parella lived through many difficulties and never seemed to be cohesive. By the end of 2006 it had contracted substantially, and because of the changes that had taken place the final operational plan was never presented to the foundation. Despite the foundation's attempts to continue, there seemed little possibility of getting the Local Support Group to agree on a way forward or even to discuss general questions, for example, whether to agree in principle to continue. YEPP-Parella was thus terminated.

Principal outcomes

Youth empowerment

As has been noted, Parella is a middle-class area with youth who can be described as disadvantaged but not genuinely 'at risk'. Generally, YEPP-Parella was not successful in involving large numbers of youth outside of the Local Support Group. Some youth became involved in the Local Support Group, but they were university students and thus exemplified the lack of 'at risk' status. The theatre project in the Cantiere Cattaneo Parella secondary school involved more youth in creating performances based on the thinking and feeling of individual youth with regard to the community.

It must be concluded that, in terms of youth empowerment, YEPP-Parella had little effect.

Community empowerment

YEPP had little or no discernible effect on community empowerment. In fact, community empowerment was never a part of the goals of the Local Support Group. In terms of community actions, YEPP did have some impact on reducing fragmentation, but this, it must be said, was not very convincing. At the outset the membership of the Local

Support Group included many different organisations, but it began in turmoil and ended as a much smaller group, still with considerable tensions and with little expectation that it would continue.

Partnerships

The independent sector

The main player in Parella was the foundation, which supported YEPP-Parella fully and worked with the public authorities. In addition, many associations and cooperatives working in the social and cultural fields were involved in the Local Support Group and they formulated and managed the various action plans. However, they never became a cohesive group and the Local Support Group did not become an actor in the local community nor, as a group, did it work with the public administration.

The public sector

Primary and secondary schools: These were involved in YEPP through the Local Support Group and in activities. The teachers on the Local Support Group brought to it substantial knowledge about the youth in Parella, with the intention of linking the school more strongly with the community. However, this vision was often not shared by the other teachers in the schools and the involvement of the schools in YEPP, in terms of numbers of students, was weak. For example, the Cantiere Cattaneo secondary school never felt fully involved and withdrew from YEPP, deciding not to renew its agreement in 2006. Overcoming this perception would have required a great deal more communication between the Local Support Group and the local coordinator and the schools.

The district: Through its president, the district fully supported YEPP, arguing that YEPP's goal of overcoming of fragmentation in services was a key aim of its youth policy. The district was represented on the Local Support Group for the first year and provided very positive support – for example, through information flow and the provision of meeting rooms. However, after a change in personnel this engagement faded out and YEPP was not involved in decision making about the opening and management of the new youth centre. Might this have been due to lack of cohesion within the Local Support Group?

The private sector

At the outset, two local shopkeepers' associations were involved with YEPP, since they felt YEPP might be able to help to overcome a general decrease in interpersonal relations in Parella. However, this involvement ended after the first year and no other private sector organisations became involved.

Trans-sectoral cooperation

Although all three sectors were involved in the development of shared projects through the action plans, as noted, there were always tensions. Additionally none of them was asked to provide its own financial resources for the YEPP work, which came in the main from the foundation. But their engagement did not last for long and many of the members withdrew, partly because their concerns were not being catered for and partly because of the perceived fragmentation of the Local Support Group and a lack of trust between its members. The rather modest success of the projects was also an impediment that reduced commitment to YEPP. Furthermore, despite an agreement on cooperation being signed between the foundation and the district, the impact was minimal. And a similar fate befell the agreement between YEPP and the Cantiere Cattaneo Parella secondary school.

Transnational cooperation

Transnational cooperation received little support from the Local Support Group and, although some youth were involved in the transnational meetings and events, YEPP-Parella benefited little from this key element of YEPP. Some members of the Local Support Group finally saw the value, but by this time the difficulties within the group were so great as to be insurmountable. Although the youth involved found the transnational meetings personally empowering and increased their confidence, and some participated in the TV transnational workshop held in Turin, YEPP-Parella did not join the EmpowerMediaNetwork and did not develop a community media project.

Sustainability

YEPP-Parella did not develop a means to create sustainability. Even after the foundation made it clear that its continued involvement was predicated on this Local Programme Site's developing its own funding. Thus, the work terminated at the end of 2006.

Policy impact

Despite the central role played by Compagnia di San Paulo in Turin and the agreement between it and the city of Turin Youth Department and Parella, there was no clear impact on local policy making.

Conclusions

Despite strong foundation support, a local coordinator and local researcher and a Local Support Group, thus fulfilling a large part of the YEPP implementation model, YEPP-Parella did not work well. The reason for this was certainly partly to do with the continuing difficult dynamics within the Local Support Group. There was a lack of trust among its members, alongside other personal difficulties. Thus, it never gelled as a team and there was weak motivation to change.

Part of this problem seems to have been due the large number of well-established independent sector groups that had their own methods of working, which would have had to change in order to work within the YEPP model. Perhaps too, the support given to the YEPP approach by the president of the district proved to be too much of a threat to the 'social services', which funded many of the independent sectors working in Parella, and implied that they were not doing a good job. It is interesting to note that this 'top-down' pressure for change is not compatible with the YEPP model, which has essentially a 'bottom-up' style of working, and this may have sent the wrong messages from the outset, leading to tensions that were never overcome and that ultimately led to disenchantment with the work.

Antwerp North, Belgium

Background

Antwerp North is a relatively large area of the city of Antwerp on the river Schelde in northern Belgium, with historic links to the port. In 2002 it had a population of 44,000.

This Local Programme Site is located in an urban area with dense, poor-quality housing, much of the property dating from the 19th century. It is currently occupied by many immigrant families, who live in houses that are in a poor state of repair, thus making it a deprived area. Incomes are lower in the Local Programme Site than in Antwerp as a whole (about 25% less), where incomes are less than in Flanders generally. In addition, there is a higher proportion of youth (35%) in Antwerp North than in Antwerp as a whole (28%). The numbers on welfare support are more than twice those for the city as a whole (5.7% versus 2.5%), as is the level of unemployment (21% versus 9.8%), with youngsters making up almost a quarter (23%) of those without jobs. Almost half of the unemployed are non-EU immigrants, many with poor levels of education.

Precursors of YEPP

Although there has been concern for the situation of children and youth in Antwerp North and there have been an array of youth services and NGO activities in the area, these activities were not coordinated and the existence of many of them was unknown to young people.

Motivation for YEPP

The lack of services and their coordination and visibility in Antwerp North, and the general level of deprivation there, became a focus for the Evens Foundation, which has its roots in Antwerp, and which decided to become more directly involved in community development work.

Structure of YEPP

The fundamentals of the YEPP structure were either not put into place or were only partially implemented. There was no Local Support Group; a local coordinator, who was unpaid for much of the time; and a local researcher, who was ignored and was also not in place for the full duration of the work. In addition, no youth were included in decision making.

What changes did YEPP bring about in Antwerp North?

Between 2002 and 2006 a nominal version of YEPP was functioning in Antwerp North. It was far from complete, and between 2002 and 2004 had only an unpaid local coordinator, who was a member of stRaten-generaal.[13] Further, throughout the duration of the work there was no Local Support Group, as defined by YEPP; no action-based operational plan was developed until 2003; and there was substantial resistance to involving the youth themselves in the planning of YEPP activities. There was continued resistance to the appointment of a local researcher by stRaten-generaal, and no inclination to take account of feedback from the researcher when this person was appointed. There was also little interest in the transnational element of YEPP. As a result, it is possible neither to describe cycles of change nor to answer the question whether YEPP 'caused' change, since the YEPP model was not fully implemented.

However, this does not mean that no progress was made in Antwerp North between 2002 and 2006, and the following sections describe the results.

First steps

In February 2002 an unpaid local coordinator was identified and the University of Antwerp was invited to become involved as an evaluation partner. The potential membership of a Local Support Group was discussed and a first operational plan was drawn up. However, this plan was a list of the strengths and weaknesses of Antwerp North and contained no proposals for action.

A secondary school providing part-time vocational training (CDO) was chosen as the central focus of YEPP work so as to provide a 'support structure for a community school', and a new operational plan was drawn up, but was not finalised until March 2003.

Public sector involvement

During this time there were meetings with public centre representatives but tensions were apparent in these discussions with regard to the style of interactions, especially between the Evens Foundation and stRaten-generaal. Thus, by October 2002 there was still no Local Support Group, no youth involvement and no action plan.

In an attempt to get things moving, a 'round table' discussion was set up involving all of the three sectors, and took place at the CDO. A new local coordinator (still unpaid) was identified and support group meetings were initiated, although these did not have YEPP's preferred structure. This support group discussed work experience issues for the most disadvantaged students at CDO and proposed a project to develop green spaces (called 'Dulomi').

Next step

In March 2003 a new operational plan was finalised. The main goal was to create 'warm-hearted neighbourhood management' via:

- the development of a framework for youth – although this did not include youth themselves and was therefore incompatible with the YEPP strategy;
- a focus on improving recreational, educational and work opportunities for youth;
- the promotion of networks of different organisations;
- the strengthening of local citizens' organisations;
- the support, training and development of work opportunities for the most disadvantaged.

Although earlier tensions over the involvement of youth and the value of transnational work continued to exist, four CDO students went to Finland to participate in the youth exchange workshop 'Music and Citizenship'. The success of this venture led, in turn, to the organisation of a transnational workshop in Antwerp in 2004.

The continuing tensions led to the disbanding of the support group – which had created this plan – in 2003. The local researcher also began to question his role, since his input was ignored. He resigned in early 2004.

Involvement of Timberland

In October 2003 the private sector company Timberland became involved and agreed to support local YEPP activities, with the result that projects were agreed with CDO. Although at first st*R*aten-generaal did not like this arrangement, it later came round to approving it.

2004: a new start

The year 2004 saw a number of new developments:

- There was a successful meeting with the National Department of Education, which came about as a result of YEPP.
- There was a second 'round table' meeting, which included youth from CDO.
- The transnational workshop took place successfully and was very much liked by the youth.
- There was a second Timberland day.

StRaten-generaal continued to resist the YEPP principles and, as a result, the local researcher resigned. The Evens Foundation then decided to use the research funds to create a position for a paid local coordinator (a position taken up by the former local researcher), and also to increase its investment in the project in Antwerp North.

At this point, in order to provide a method for carrying out the situational analysis, the Evens Foundation decided to invite RISO (Antwerp's centre for community development) to become involved. RISO was already supporting a project called Buurtschatten[14] that was based on the Scarman Trust's 'Can Do' method. The additional connection with the Scarman Trust via a seminar on the 'Can Do' method in February 2005 also had a strong impact on the Buurtschatten project.

In 2004 a new operational plan was prepared. This focused on the most disadvantaged youngsters at CDO and had two aims: first, to create more educational and employment opportunities for them, and second, to expand recreational possibilities for young people in Antwerp North. It identified nine projects, many of which were supported by both the public and private sectors. Of the nine projects, the first five were aimed at employment and the remaining four at recreation. They were:

- additional training for members of the 'remaining group', intended to create better attitudes and self-image and to give them new skills;
- 'What a match', to provide work experience opportunities for young people to work with senior citizens (over 80 years old);
- renovation project, to create regular employment positions and provide opportunities for the development of new skills;
- practice job applications at Timberland, to stress the importance of language, attitudes and dress at job interviews;
- 'greenery training', for work experience opportunities and to create regular employment;
- community TV, to give young people the chance to showcase their community;
- support for the CDO football team, to provide social opportunities, recreation, instil a 'winning' frame of mind, make YEPP visible and create a 'billboard' for the school;
- support for Buurtschatten via a network and focusing on young people;
- creation of a public park for the school and neighbourhood, and as work experience.

During the creation of this plan there were further discussions about establishing a Local Support Group. However, this did not come about and the group came to an end after two meetings in 2005. In addition, the local coordinator became the de facto manager of the projects after being taken on as an employee by the Evens Foundation.

The nine projects identified in the 2004 action plan formed the basis of the work in Antwerp North in the following two years. One feature was strong collaboration between the CDO and the public sector, and continued work with Timberland. Antwerp North was also involved in the EmpowerMediaNetwork element of the transnational work. The projects themselves developed somewhat independently and with different degrees of success and were supported by YEPP, but were far from meeting the full set of YEPP criteria.

Despite the slow progress, 2007 saw further developments in Antwerp North;

• The Evens Foundation committed funding for several more years.
• With stimulus from an initiative taken by the Local Programme Site in Tuzla-Simin Han, a community fund was established in collaboration with RISO and an anonymous foundation (including Evens) in order to support micro-projects in Antwerp North. A management board was formed, composed of local residents, that included three young people, one of whom was aged 18.

Comment

It is clear from the account given above that a strong form of YEPP was not implemented in Antwerp North and therefore little can be concluded about whether YEPP caused the changes that took place. Nevertheless, it was also clear that there were changes consistent with YEPP's philosophy of involving different sectors in community development and of the impact of transnational collaboration. The impact of the latter was seen especially in the involvement of Antwerp North in the EmpowerMediaNetwork, and also in the creation of the community fund. The YEPP work also impacted on the Evens Foundation, which later decided to create new programme sites in other countries in which it works, such as Poland. It seems unlikely that this would have happened without the Foundation's involvement in YEPP.

Principal outcomes

Youth empowerment

Involvement in community TV via the EmpowerMediaNetwork provided an opportunity for empowerment by facilitating young people's participation in decision making, and also by bringing together different elements of society that normally have little opportunity to interact with each other. The sailing boat project, which provides opportunities for young offenders to reflect on their lives in a different context, may have potential. The transnational youth workshop also gave young people an opportunity to develop constructive proposals for change, by presenting and defending them in a public setting.

Community empowerment

CDO was identified at the outset as the key community partner, and involvement in YEPP has enhanced its reputation – for example, through the participation of Timberland – and increased its influence with city officials. The fact that, by the end of the work in Antwerp North, the CDO felt that it no longer needed YEPP perhaps indicates the impact of the empowerment process adopted by YEPP. This evaluation must be tempered, however, by the observation that CDO ultimately did not open its doors to the community in Antwerp North, and thus this potential element of empowerment was lost.

The Asset-Based Community Development approach, which involved RISO and the Buurtschatten project, became central to YEPP's work in Antwerp North in 2004. The work has led to a number of innovations, such as the sailing boat project and the new children's centre, which provide new opportunities for young people.

Despite these developments, Antwerp North still lacks a structure such as a Local Support Group for planning, coordinating and implementing community change actions. The structure of the community fund perhaps offers some possibilities in this area.

Partnerships

The independent sector

The leading organisations were the Evens Foundation, the Bernheim Foundation and stRaten-generaal. The Evens Foundation became the main independent sector partner in Antwerp North and has increased its financial commitment over the duration of the project.

Now it is committed to developing sustainability there. The Bernheim Foundation has played a lesser role but made the very important contact with Timberland. Despite these successes, the link with stRaten-generaal was not successful, mainly because its approach was not commensurate with that of YEPP. Since 2004 there has been increasing commitment to involving more independent sector organisations, such as Hoger Wal[15] and the community fund.

The public sector

Support from the city of Antwerp was rather weak at the beginning, but increased over time. Some projects have been implemented with support from city councillors. RISO has become a partner of YEPP, and together they have promoted, for instance, the sailing boat project and the community fund. However, links with other public services such as OCMW[16] did not develop so well. Policy decisions made by the city of Antwerp were also detrimental, since one led to a reduction in funding and another negatively affected the work of many community organisations.

CDO-Noord: The school was YEPP's main partner at the outset and this led to some joint projects that provided work experience for disadvantaged youth. Since its earlier commitment to community involvement, the school's stance has changed and, despite support for renewing the sports hall and the park next door to the school, neither facility is open to local residents.

The private sector

Timberland, through its 'Serv-a-palooza-Day' programme, has supported the school by bringing its own staff together with the teachers and students to carry out certain projects such as the renewal of the school sports hall. The Timberland staff working in the school inspired students and opened their minds to new aspirations. However, despite efforts to increase the involvement of Timberland, the relationship has remained at the level of just one day a year.

Trans-sectoral cooperation

The cooperation between the foundations, CDO-Noord and Timberland is a rare example of trans-sectoral cooperation in the YEPP work. Since 2004 this cooperation has strengthened and has led to some long-term strategic partnerships, especially with RISO.

However, since there was no Local Support Group there is no means to reflect in a holistic way on the developments in Antwerp North as a Local Programme Site.

Transnational cooperation

Transnational cooperation, which is central to YEPP, began in a very limited way and met with considerable resistance from stRaten-generaal. However, as time passed, youth in Antwerp North did become more connected with youth in other Local Programme Sites, especially in the EmpowerMediaNetwork. The development of the community fund was inspired by innovations in Tuzla-Simin Han, and was learnt about through the transnational programme of YEPP.

Sustainability

The Evens Foundation remains committed to the work in Antwerp North and the continued involvement of the public sector through RISO and the development of the community fund will be key elements of future work.

Policy impact

Towards the end of YEPP I in Antwerp North, some public sector organisations such as RISO became partners and were involved in the development of the nine projects of the last action plan. Whether this experience has impacted on their policy making is unclear. Otherwise, there seems to have been little effect, with many promises fading away and a lack of evident action on the ground. The city of Antwerp has not become involved. It must be concluded that the impact on policy making was weak, at best.

Conclusions

It is clear from both the internal and external evaluations that Antwerp North did not implement the YEPP model, and thus no strong conclusions can be drawn as to whether YEPP caused changes there. However, it is clear that there were substantial and sustainable changes in Antwerp North that are known about because of YEPP's involvement and its monitoring process.

There is evidence that the transnational component was especially influential and impacted on developments in Antwerp North, especially EmpowerMediaNetwork and the initiation of the community fund.

It is clear that the involvement with stRaten-generaal was not a successful partnership, since its strategy and style was strongly at odds with the YEPP model. The tensions that inevitably emerged were counter-productive. In addition, the Evens Foundation's lack of experience in community work in the beginning led to less than full financial commitment at the outset. This was resolved later on and the Foundation's increasing involvement clearly contributed positively to the implementation of the work.

Mannheim – Neckarstadt-West, Germany

Background

Neckarstadt-West is a part of the Neckarstadt, which, in turn, is one of the 17 districts of the city of Mannheim, Germany. Mannheim (population 323,736) is located in the industrial heartland of western Germany in the Rhine-Neckar region, and has an important inland port.

Neckarstadt-West is an urban area with a working-class population that, at the time of the study, had a high concentration of unemployment, with 41% immigrant workers, twice that of the city's average of 20%. The majority of immigrants come from Muslim countries, especially Turkey.

The major issues facing youth in Neckarstadt-West are:

- lack of knowledge of the German language;
- lack of access to the city's youth support structure;
- poor preparation for vocational training;
- shortage of places in the dual system of vocational training.

Precursors of YEPP

For many years, Mannheim has been promoting projects to support disadvantaged citizens, which have been supported by the Freudenberg Foundation. Thus, when YEPP was initiated in Mannheim Neckarstadt-West, it is not surprising that the programme was located within the existing structure of the Intercultural Education Centre/Project (IKUBIZ), created in 1983.

Motivation for YEPP

Since 2000, the city of Mannheim has been expanding its initiatives to create activities and employment. It is combining training and job creation with the improvement of security and property in the most difficult of the town's districts. It has a strategy of developing holistic employability programmes for young people in these districts.

Structure of YEPP

YEPP in Neckarstadt-West has a local coordinator and a researcher, but no Local Support Group. Additionally, no youth were involved in decision making.

What changes did YEPP bring about in Neckarstadt-West?

Between 2001 and 2006 a nominal version of YEPP was functioning in Neckarstadt-West. It is important to stress that this version of YEPP was far from complete. Although there were local coordinators and there was substantial collaboration between the public and independent sectors, the YEPP implementation lacked a Local Support Group and full evaluation. There was unwillingness to listen to feedback from the researcher, a lack of acceptance of the action research model and, for a long time, no commitment to the transnational element of YEPP. As a result, it is possible neither to describe cycles of change nor to answer the question whether or not YEPP 'caused' change, since the YEPP model was not fully implemented.

However, this does not mean that no progress was made in Neckarstadt-West, and the following sections organise information around operational plans as they occurred, more or less chronologically, and then describe the main outcomes.

First operational plan developed, 2001
Step 1
It was agreed to pursue four important areas:

- entrepreneurship (ProFiMa)
- intercultural dialogue with Islam
- learning democracy
- the Community Art Centre.

Step 2

A cross-sectoral meeting described as the 'YEPP Supporters' Group' was established. This group was not the equivalent of YEPP's Local Support Group, since, for instance, it had no representation of local young people. The group comprised senior officials of the city of Mannheim, the supporting foundation and IKUBIZ and set out to determine an overall strategy. Nevertheless, it had a critical influence on developments in Neckarstadt-West by allowing the foundation to bring YEPP to the attention of the city administration, which led to a local coordinator being identified.

Spring 2002: second meeting of YEPP Supporters' Group

The following were outcomes of this meeting:

- it identified the YEPP site in Mannheim as Neckarstadt-West;
- a local researcher was appointed;
- the first operational plan was revised and confirmed, focusing on:
  - improvement of linguistic competence;
  - empowerment of individual and group initiatives;
  - development of new instruments for local community building in Neckarstadt-West.

The meeting also agreed to stress the importance of involving local actors as a quality criterion, and a cooperation agreement was signed between YEPP and the city of Mannheim (Office of Culture) to start cultural projects in Neckarstadt-West.

July 2002: third meeting of YEPP Supporters' Group

Language training for young people with migrant backgrounds was identified as a key theme for YEPP.

First projects in Neckarstadt-West

- Background work was carried out by the local coordinator and agreements were made with local actors on the themes identified.
- In September 2002 the operational plan was updated and endorsed by the Mayor.
- Working groups composed of individual actors were established for each of the themes. These working groups were substitutes for the Local Support Group.
- A new part-time local coordinator was appointed.

October 2002: fourth YEPP Supporters' Group

- The 'Backpack'[17] concept for language training was proposed.
- The fifth meeting of the group was planned for December, but it was cancelled. This marked the decline of the strategic public-independent sector partnership.
- However, a Neighbourhood Management team was established in Neckarstadt-West with the city and other social welfare agencies. It had strong support from the Freudenberg Foundation, and it was intended to develop a holistic approach.

During winter 2002/03, YEPP was presented to the public sector groups and well received by the mayor. But Neckarstadt-West agreed to hold back from transnational involvement, even though the mayor was especially interested in this theme.

2003–04

- The YEPP Neckarstadt-West newsletter was started.
- Agreed projects developed in collaboration with the public sector, but independently, not holistically, for instance:
  - *Community art:* Within the context of broader project goals, YEPP in Neckarstadt-West focused on 'the fostering of personal initiative and social responsibility through project work with artists' in photography, video, film, drama, dance and painting. This led to a 2-day workshop to develop projects. Nine projects were identified, each with a working group. These produced outcomes and led to the creation of a website in the summer of 2003.
- A YEPP office was opened in Neckarstadt-West (2003). There was an opening ceremony with the mayor and the chairman of the Freudenberg Foundation.
- In the autumn of 2003 there was a closed meeting to discuss the operational plan for 2004.
- This led to the opening of a shop to display artwork in Neckarstadt-West. A photography project developed, as well as the idea for a Neckarstadt-West musical. The Art Shop became independent in 2004 and continued into 2005, funded by the city, the Freudenberg Foundation and URBAN II (EU).

Backpack: Three day-care facilities were involved, but this was an IKUBIZ pilot project and YEPP was in partnership with the city and the university and German Language Institute. Six to 10 parents were involved in each day-care facility. This was successful and was later expanded within the city.

Reading Shop: This grew out of Backpack and led to the establishment of a centre in Neckarstadt-West with funding and staff from IKUBIZ.

Learning responsibility/service learning: These actions were implemented in collaboration with the Office for Education, IKUBIZ and the university. Mentoring programmes were developed between schools in, for example, reading and homework. This work continued with 'Campus Aktiv'.

Neighbourhood management
- In May 2004 neighbourhood management was launched in Neckarstadt-West, funded by the Freudenberg Foundation, but in collaboration with YEPP. An executive group was created by the supporting foundation – the so-called 'Kuchenkabinet' – with offices shared initially with YEPP.
- The neighbourhood management approach in Neckarstadt-West was influenced by YEPP's guiding philosophy.
- A community assembly formed through neighbourhood management identified a number of issues to work on through working groups.
- The YEPP local coordinators worked with the neighbourhood management team as moderators of working groups on youth and education.

Transnational involvement
Some involvement in 2003 and 2004. Only one of the local coordinators took part, presumably because he could speak English, and there was some involvement of Neckarstadt-West youth but also some dissatisfaction.

Year 4: 2005
All projects continued.

Backpack: This programme was extended and expanded and was the only project that was evaluated by the local researcher. Her evaluations were found to be very useful and helped in the extension of the project.

Reading Shop: This programme developed into a parents' school, run in collaboration with the public sector. A plan was prepared to give future responsibility for the 'shop' to mothers. However, the local coordinator was involved in only a minimal way.

Learning responsibility: This programme was extended and continued with the Humboldt lower secondary school and the Neckar primary school, with the Hilda lower secondary school joining in for some activities. Leisure-time activities were developed and were well structured. The learning responsibility project was divided into two levels – mentoring at school level and new courses at the university pedagogical training level. But there was no connection with IKUBIZ or YEPP.

ProFi Lease Office and ProFi Junior: These programmes began only in 2004 with ProFi Mannheim and a competition to create and support pupils and youth companies. There was some involvement of the private sector and ProFi Junior cooperated with YEPP.

Youth culture and youth media work: This programme made a documentary on Neckarstadt-West, a musical ('Neckarstadt-West Side Story') and participated in the EmpowerMediaNetwork. The musical received support from the public, private and independent sectors.

Transnational involvement: The first involvement in these activities since 2002 was initiated. But Neckarstadt-West local coordinators did not attend the YEPP transnational local coordinators' meeting held in Neckarstadt-West!

2006–07

During this period,

- local researcher's position was not continued;
- projects continued and some expanded, for example:
  - ProFi Lease Office and ProFi Junior;
  - youth culture and media work;
  - first transnational youth exchange workshop held.

Comment

It is clear from the outline presented above that the YEPP implementation in Neckarstadt-West was far from complete, and therefore it is not possible to comment on the causal impact of YEPP in this site. It could well have been that any funded, holistic programme that benefited from the continuity of foundation support would have worked equally well. However, there are hints from the external evaluation that YEPP did help to change attitudes and that the transnational component of YEPP, although initially rejected, did lead to new thinking.

Principal outcomes

Youth empowerment

Language training through Backpack: This programme was evaluated by the local researcher and led to improvements in both German and Turkish languages and improved social skills, creating more self-assured child–adult and child–child interactions. Changes were also observed in mothers, in terms of their confidence and German language skills and understanding of the demands of German education.

Reading Shop: The mothers involved acquired new skills, knowledge and self-esteem. The Reading Shop became a base for the self-organisation of women in Neckarstadt-West.

Learning responsibility: Children and young people at school were given the opportunity to participate actively in responding to local needs and finding solutions. These included: handling conflict in school, homework assistance, developing reading competence, support for exam preparation, more leisure-time activities and an understanding of children's rights.

Campus Aktiv: The university students involved also benefited through this authentic experience.

ProFi junior: This programme gave young people the opportunity to formulate business ideas via a competition, 'Your idea – You are the boss', and it strongly supported the winners of the competition. Involvement led to increased motivation in school and stressed the importance of taking responsibility for one's own life.

Youth cultural work: This aimed to promote youth empowerment through project work with artists – for example, sculpture and theatre.

Comment

However, it should be noted that these projects were loosely connected with each other and youth were not involved in the overall planning of YEPP activities.

Community empowerment

Community empowerment was not stressed by YEPP Neckarstadt-West and it was not until the neighbourhood management scheme was established that this became more important.

Language training through Backpack: This extended to the training of kindergarten teachers, helped to enhance the education offered and had an impact on the community.

Reading Shop: This has become indispensable in the community for social coexistence and lifelong learning. It concentrated community resources and has contributed to intercultural development, social integration and sustainability.

Learning responsibility: The involvement of the university was a very important factor and has helped to give continuity to the project.

ProFi junior and ProFi lease office: These programmes have helped to bring youth companies into existence and to create contact with schools, facilities and other businesses, which has helped to strengthen the district's social capital.

Culture: Projects carried out in the cultural arena have helped to strengthen the district's communication and networking facilities, fostering identification with Neckarstadt-West and enabling equal opportunity. The Art Shop was set up through collaboration between YEPP and the city's Office for Culture. It has become a venue for a range of artistic and cultural activities, further strengthening social capital.

The link between youth and community empowerment

YEPP focused on youth and neighbourhood management in the community. This collaboration has great potential for an integrated approach that could be mutually beneficial, as has been seen in the Reading Shop, the Art Shop and ProFi Lease Office, which now form part of the Neckarstadt-West community and did not exist before. In future, this approach could be expanded so as to include more youth in the decision-making processes.

Partnerships

The independent sector

The leading organisations were the Freudenberg Foundation and the Intercultural Centre (IKUBIZ), which housed YEPP. They also pressed for the establishment of neighbourhood management. IKUBIZ also committed to YEPP and supported, for example, the Backpack project and the Reading Shop. The social-pedagogical project (QUIST) was also involved. There were also other partners, for example, the service agency of the Protestant Church and other independent groups such as local artists. All of these groups also supported neighbourhood management.

The public sector

Federal/Land: Public sector officials at the federal level were well aware of the problems related to youth integration and immigration and of the need, for instance, of integrated policy-making, yet they felt powerless to do anything, especially in the context of the structure and organisation of the large German government bureaucracy. There is little or no evidence that these officials were influenced by YEPP.

Local: A general cooperation agreement between the Freudenberg Foundation and the city of Mannheim was entered into at the outset. It led to a successful proposal to the EC for financial support. However, in time it became clear that some departments in the city were more committed than others, and there was a general lack of engagement on the part of the mayor. There was cooperation with Youth, Social Affairs, Health, Culture and Education, and also with the department responsible for kindergartens and with the Commissioners for Foreign Residents and Municipal Employment Promotion.

The private sector

This sector was involved in sponsoring some of the activities, such as the theatre, but not in the planning phase. Networking and dissemination activities developed by neighbourhood management facilitated the involvement of businesses.

Trans-sectoral cooperation

Where this happened, it was embedded in the cooperation agreement between the city and the Freudenberg Foundation. There was cooperation in learning responsibility, ProFi Junior, language training and culture. This cooperation was mainly between the public and independent sectors, with the private sector providing some financial support.

YEPP also played a significant part in setting up neighbourhood management and reinforcing activities related to empowerment and collaboration, and new forms of cooperation.

Transnational cooperation

This was weak, with little impact on local activities, although later on in the project there was active engagement with the EmpowerMediaNetwork.

Sustainability

The keys to sustainability in Neckarstadt-West are the continued involvement of the Freudenberg Foundation and the links with the city and the establishment of neighbourhood management. Sustaining the developments in Neckarstadt-West would certainly be facilitated by establishing the Reading Shop and the Art Shop on a more permanent basis.

Policy impact

Although YEPP was incompletely implemented, there does appear to have been some spin-off effect on the neighbourhood management scheme that was introduced in Neckarstadt-West. But the evidence for this claim is not strong and the scheme could well have taken the form that it did within any community development approach that stressed partnerships.

Conclusions

It is very clear from both the internal and external evaluations that Neckarstadt-West in Mannheim did not implement the YEPP model in full. Thus, no hard conclusion can be drawn that YEPP caused change there. However, it is clear that there were substantial and sustainable changes in Neckarstadt-West, which are known about in some detail because of the YEPP internal evaluation framework. The one activity that was evaluated more formally ('Backpack') provided very useful information to help in extending that work. This being noted, it must also be said that other projects were also extended. without a more formal evaluation.

There is some evidence that the conceptual elements of YEPP, particularly its holist approach and the transnational component, were influential and impacted, respectively, on the way that the neighbourhood management was set up and, eventually, on involving Neckarstadt-West more fully in cultural developments.

Otherwise, it is possible only to speculate as to why the YEPP model was not fully implemented. Housing it within an on-going project, IKUBIZ, with an established routine and style of work certainly did not help. From the outset there was also a very strong link with the public sector, which has a long history through the work of the Freudenberg Foundation. This again may have prevented the participants involved in YEPP from establishing the YEPP approach and creating ownership. For example, many of the projects that started up ran relatively independently of one another, each associated with a different public sector administration, and many never became strongly identified with YEPP. The work in Neckarstadt-West never involved the youth themselves in the decision-making process, a central tenet of YEPP. As a consequence, the opportunity to create conditions to promote this element of youth empowerment through YEPP was largely lost.

The newcomer

Dublin North East Inner City, Ireland

Background

Dublin's North East Inner City is an area of 6.38 square kilometres in the centre of Dublin, the capital city of Ireland. It comprises 10 electoral divisions and has a population of 4,800 per square kilometre. It has regularly been identified as one of the most deprived areas of the country. More recently, government- and privately funded building and refurbishment schemes have led to improvements. As a result, the demographics have changed and, with recent immigration from a wide range of countries, there is now a rather heterogeneous population. Following these changes, the level of wealth has been slowly increasing, but there remain pockets of deprivation and poverty, poor levels of education, and social exclusion, with the consequences that this entails, such as unemployment, drug trafficking and so on.

Precursors of YEPP

The North East Inner City (NEIC) has a long history of community development based on the creation of partnerships between the statutory bodies and the local community, including the private and independent sectors. For instance, the Dublin Inner City Partnership is a company that brings representatives of the community and voluntary sector together with the public and private sectors. It is a leading agency in implementing the local development programme, especially in tackling long-term unemployment. The partnership is community led and its projects are developed through local actions and networks. The Inner City Organisations Network (ICON) is responsible for NEIC. ICON has a holistic approach and has worked over many years to integrate services for children and youth at risk, leading eventually to the establishment of the Young People at Risk (YPAR) structure within which YEPP in the Dublin North East Inner City programme site worked.

Motivation for YEPP

Dublin North East Inner City joined the YEPP structure in 2004 in order to provide additional impetus to the on-going activities that were supporting young people at risk. The main goal was to accelerate the integration of the statutory services in support of children, youth and families at risk, in order to increase the efficiency of the services provided. The reputation of the partners, especially the OECD, was also an important influence for Dublin North East Inner City with regard to impact on policy.

Structure of YEPP

YEPP had a local coordinator and researcher. In addition, there was a Local Support Group. Young people were also included.

What changes did YEPP bring about in Dublin North East Inner City?

YEPP began its work in Dublin North East Inner City in 2004 and essentially brought its transnational programme to support and complement the on-going work of ICON/YPAR. YEPP was perceived to be the same project as YPAR, although in practice and as viewed locally the transnational part of the work was YEPP, while the local implementation was YPAR. In January 2004 the first Local Support Group[18] was established under the auspices of the Local Child Protection Committee, with ICON being identified as the lead agency. A local researcher was appointed, and a local coordinator was also appointed much later in the year.

Perhaps because of the long history of community work in Dublin North East Inner City and because YEPP was embedded in YPAR, the YEPP development model involving cycles of development was eventually initiated through a detailed context analysis that led to a great deal of reflection on what to do, how to do it and whom to include. Leading up to this there was agreement on the geographical area that would make up the Local Programme Site and on the structures and relationships with the Local Child Protection Committee (NAHB). A Local Support Group was established with wide representation from the public and independent sectors and young people.

2004: first decisions of the Local Support Group
Goals:
- to provide an effective response to the issue of young people at risk in the Local Programme Site;
- to ensure that there was an appropriate level of accurate and timely information;
- to ensure that the necessary structures, mechanisms and protocols were in place.

Means
- Three groups were set up covering young people in the age groups 0–5, 6–12 and 13–18 whose representatives were able to provide input into the YPAR process.
- A sub-committee was established to explore the best models and practices for consulting and involving young people in the process.

Results
A number of transnational visits were made that included young people.

2005
A number of working groups were established in 2005.

Goals:
- *0–5 years:* Work with parents to identify children and family needs.
- *After-school provision:* This focused on the provision of local after-school activities.
- *Needs of foreign-national young people:* Seminars led to the forwarding of specific recommendations to a number of public sector agencies, NGOs and other groups.
- *Out of hours work with young people and the needs of 'unattached' youth:* This focused on the needs of youth at risk and the provision of core youth services out of hours and at weekends.

- *Respite care*: Identified the need for respite care in families most at risk. Local projects with the local drug task force had been initiated.
- *Structures for the participation of young people in YPAR*: This made plans to establish a teenage organisation in 2006 to develop an action plan.
- *'The voice of the child' – consultation with pre-teens*: Consultations had taken place, focusing on the lack of provision of activities for children aged under 10 and the use of local play areas and facilities.

Results:

- A report was prepared mapping the voluntary/community groups and statutory agencies already working in the Dublin North East Inner City programme site.
- A seminar concerning young foreign nationals took place.
- There was involvement in the transnational work.

2006

A strategic plan was presented in 2006 at a meeting at which the Irish Prime Minister was present.

The mission of YPAR is to:

- establish an integrated, interagency structure;
- improve the quality and delivery of services;
- establish appropriate mechanisms to coordinate and integrate services;
- support young people in accessing services, education, training and employment;
- ensure anti-discriminatory and accessible policies and practices in services;
- provide support to develop the skills and capacities needed for young people to become active members of the community;
- ensure that the voices and views of young people at risk are heard;
- evaluate the intervention from the very beginning, in order to monitor progress and learn what works and what does not work.

The goals of YPAR are to:

- map existing services for young people at risk in the NEIC and identify gaps in service provision;
- develop, promote, advocate and evaluate the YPAR plan;
- develop responses to the identified and emerging needs of young people at risk;

- facilitate the participation of young people and their families in the development of services in the community;
- develop common protocols to facilitate the integration of service provision;
- document and disseminate examples of best practice in interagency service delivery for young people at risk;
- participate in YEPP's transnational initiatives focused on promoting youth empowerment.

Comment

YEPP's work in the North East Inner City area of Dublin started rather late in the history of the whole YEPP project and was heavily influenced by the organisations and structures that were already in place. During the on-going ground clearing undertaken by the Local Support Group, and which occupied much of the period 2004–06, only a rudimentary version of YEPP was put in place. This led to strong engagement in the transnational work and paved the way for the first action plan in 2006. Involvement in the transnational programme was viewed by those in Dublin North East Inner City as the main element of YEPP.

Principal outcomes

Youth empowerment

The involvement of YEPP in YPAR created pressure to include more young people in the decision-making processes. In order to achieve this, a working group on youth participation was established by the Local Support Group. According to some of the young people involved, YEPP has provided a platform for them to express their views, work together in groups and communicate their priorities and wishes for the community. These opportunities have been very much appreciated. The young people liked the direct approach and the transparency of the process. In addition, the consultation process, which is leading to the development of a Youth Forum, is regarded as being very important. Being on the Local Support Group is also seen as empowering, as is the transnational involvement. During the period in which YEPP was working in Dublin North East Inner City, increasing numbers of youth became involved in YEPP, for instance in the EmpowerMediaNetwork.

Community empowerment

One of the main achievements was the completion of a community mapping exercise. This piece of research identified strengths and weaknesses in the overall community provision, thus identifying areas in need of development. This work influenced the strategic plan that was constructed for YPAR. Involvement in the transnational project also helped those involved in YEPP to address the challenge of integrating foreign nationals into the community by meeting real people rather than dealing with stereotypes.

Cultural events such as street art were also promoted and these, alongside involvement in the EmpowerMediaNetwork to create community TV, also helped to empower the community.

Partnerships

The independent sector

YEPP in Dublin North East Inner City benefited from strong support from the independent sector, especially from the Irish Youth Foundation and the Charles Stewart Mott Foundation.

The public sector

Representatives of the public sector took part regularly in the Local Support Group meetings. However, some ministries were easier to involve than others. For example, the Ministry of Health was a regular participant, but bringing the Department of Education and Science to the table proved more difficult.

The private sector

There was little or no involvement of the private sector.

Trans-sectoral cooperation

Most cooperation and activity was between the statutory and voluntary sectors, including the independent sector. There was little involvement of the private sector.

Transnational cooperation

The Dublin North East Inner City Local Support Group actively engaged in YEPP and attended transnational events in Antwerp, Turin and Berlin and hosted a local coordinators' meeting. The young people reported that being selected to travel and going on their own was an important experience. Furthermore, opportunities to express their views at workshops and to meet youth from other cultures were also greatly valued.

There is some evidence that skills were enhanced, especially by involvement in community TV. Social skills were also improved, especially learning how to communicate with non-English speakers.

Sustainability

The planning work that took place during the first two years by a committed Local Support Group, representing many different bodies and with vast experience, and that culminated in the presentation of the YPAR mission and goals to the Taoiseach (prime minister of Ireland), is viewed as laying important foundations for the future. The availability through YEPP of new funding from the independent sectors should also assist in maintaining a context of sustainability, especially if this can be linked with public sector support.

Policy impact

Since YEPP has had a somewhat short life in Dublin North East Inner City, and within a rather complex context, it is difficult to judge its policy impact. Clearly, the formal recognition of YPAR (of which YEPP was a part) by the Taoiseach was a major development, and the process may well have been accelerated by the involvement in YEPP.

Conclusions

It is clear that YEPP was not realised in any strong form in Dublin North East Inner City, and therefore few definite conclusions can be drawn about its impact. With the launching of YPAR, the work may just be on the point of taking off. Certainly, the transnational component of YEPP was fully appreciated by the youth who took part and of course this would not have happened without YEPP.

Notes

[1] The case study reports of the internal evaluation for each Local Programme Site, available from the YEPP International Resource Centre (YEPP IRC), Berlin; and the OECD external evaluation, *Promoting partnerships for inclusion* EDU/CERI/PPP (2007), Paris: OECD. Available also at: www.yepp-community.org/10 Years of YEPP/YEPP Phase I.

[2] IPAK translates as 'Nevertheless' (in German, *Trotzdem*) and is a youth initiative founded in Germany in 1995 in response to the massacre in Tuzla on 25 May 1995, in which 71 young people died and more than 265 young people were injured. It supports youth initiatives, vocational training and youth peace work in Tuzla.

[3] From October 2002 onwards, five local volunteers funded by the Youth Volunteers' Programme of the Robert Bosch Foundation were actively involved in YEPP Simin Han.

[4] The donors were the International Rescue Committee (IRC) (funding the green area around the Agora); American Development Fund (for the Safe Children in Traffic campaign), also funded by Bospo (a national NGO); Dumfries and Galloway Action/Scotland funded the Youth Bank, led by the Community Foundation; Charles Stewart Mott Foundation (leadership training, Community Foundation empowerment, transnational exchanges of staff, production of promotional materials).

[5] These are interviews intended to motivate citizens to participate and become involved in change.

[6] Can Do is a working method to help communities develop action plans that was developed by the Scarman Trust.

[7] This is training for youngsters on how to create a digital container in order to promote reading and writing through new media.

[8] There were two local programme sites in Turin, in Mirafiori and Parella.

[9] METODI was the name of a company that was providing training courses for YEPP members in Turin.

[10] YEPP was renamed MiraYEPP around this time – indicative of increased ownership of YEPP, and perhaps to distinguish it from YEPP in Parella.

[11] The Little Parliament was derived from school-based pupils' councils. It has power to allocate funds for youth project proposals.

[12] The YEPP evaluation ceased in December 2005 and no data are available from which to provide the results.

[13] St*R*aten-generaal is a citizens' initiative that was established in the late 1990s as a protest movement against the planned removal of trees in Antwerp for road reconstruction. Most of its members have professional backgrounds (for example, lawyers, teachers) and the group has become well known for its ability to build strong, yet partly informal, networks to oppose mainstream policies. Its name is a play on words, based on the 'staten generaal', meaning the assembly of states that was established in 1815 as the national parliament of the then joint state of Belgium and the Netherlands. By including the letter 'R' in the name the Flemish word for streets (*straten*) is formed, thus evoking the idea of a political movement 'from the streets'. The '*R*' in italics stresses st*R*aten-generaal's opposition to perceived undemocratic decision-making procedures. YEPP began its work in Antwerp-North through collaboration with st*R*aten-generaal, which had been a partner with the Evens Foundation beforehand and was funded for this purpose by the Foundation to coordinate the local programme from 2002 to 2004. The collaboration was terminated in 2005.

[14] Buurtschatten, literally 'the treasures of the neighbourhood', is a project aiming to encourage and support all kinds of initiatives set up by the inhabitants of the Local Programme Site.

[15] Hoger Wal is a project supported by the Evens Foundation that provides sailing boat experiences for young people in problematic situations.

[16] The main public service in Belgium offering services for the elderly.

[17] Backpack is a language training scheme for non-native speakers of German.

[18] The main members of the local support group were the Northern Area Health Board (NAHB); ICON; the National Education Welfare Board; the Irish Youth Foundation; the city of Dublin Youth Services Board; the Department of Education and Science; and two members from each of the three Age Groups. The local support group met twice per month and was co-chaired by a member of ICON and the Health Board Child Care Manager.

FOUR

YEPP I: meeting the goals

This chapter presents the data from the Local Programme Sites described in Chapter Three, in tabular form, and provides further discussion, especially from a comparative perspective. In these tables the seven Local Programme Sites have been grouped together on the basis of how well they implemented the YEPP model and met the 10 non-negotiable elements of YEPP. Thus, Tuzla-Simin Han, Mirafiori and Kristinestad are considered 'well implemented' and Parella, Antwerp North and Mannheim Neckarstadt-West as 'partly implemented'. Dublin North East Inner City is treated individually because it was a latecomer to the YEPP. These tables provide 'at a glance' indications of hundreds of pages of reports and observations and analysis gathered over the course of YEPP I. They give indications on:

- The extent to which YEPP's 10 non-negotiable principles were adhered to (Table 4.1);
- How far the principal features of YEPP's research structure were implemented (Table 4.2);
- The main outcomes – relating to:
    - youth and community empowerment (Table 4.3);
    - partnerships (Table 4.4);
    - transnational activities (Table 4.5);
    - sustainability issues in each site (Table 4.6);
    - the impact on public policy (Table 4.7); and
    - a summary of the impacts of well- and partly implemented sites (Table 4.8).

Table 4.1: The extent to which YEPP's 10 non-negotiable principles were met by the Local Programme Sites

	YEPP well-implemented			YEPP partly implemented			Newcomer to YEPP
	Tuzla-Simin Han	Turin-Mirafiori	Kristinestad	Turin-Parella	Antwerp North	Mannheim Neckarstadt-West	Dublin North East Inner City*
Local needs and resources (1)	++	++	++	+	+	++	++
Cross-sectoral partnerships (2)	++ Independent – public-private	+ Independent – public Limited Private	+ Independent – public Limited private	+ Independent – public Limited private	+ Independent – public-private	+ Independent – public Limited private	+ Independent – public
Local stakeholders involved (3)	++	++	++	++	++	++	++
Active participation of youth (4)	++	++	++	+	?	?	++
Integrating action and evaluation (5)	++	++	+	++	X	?	+
Bridging gaps between schools, youth and community (6)	++	+	++	++	+	++	?
Investing in youth capacity (7)	++	++	++	++	+	+	++
Equal opportunities (8)	++	++	++	?	?	++	++
Integrating local and transnational work (9)	++	++	++	?	?	?	+
Advocacy for new policies (10)	++	+	++	X	+	+	++

Notes: Dublin North East Inner City* = 2004–06; ++ = strong involvement; + = average involvement; ? = little or uncertain involvement; X = no involvement

The extent to which YEPP's 10 non-negotiable principles were adhered to

As noted, Table 4.1 gives an indication of the extent to which each of the Local Programme Sites involved in YEPP adhered to YEPP's fundamental principles. Using these criteria it is interesting to note that only three sites, Tuzla-Simin Han, Mirafiori and Kristinestad, comply with all 10 principles and thus are the only fully implemented sites. They have mainly two '+' signs in each cell and no '?s' or 'Xs'. Dublin North East Inner City and Parella, Antwerp North and Mannheim Neckarstadt-West have many '+' signs but also many '?' signs in key areas. For instance Antwerp North and Mannheim Neckarstadt-West had low involvement of youth in decision making (4), difficulties in integrating action and evaluation (5) and were poor on investing in young people's capacities (7). Parella and Antwerp North also made less progress in providing equal opportunities (8) within YEPP. Parella, Antwerp North and Mannheim Neckarstadt-West also had difficulty in integrating local and transnational work (9) and, finally, Parella had little or no impact on public policy. Despite Dublin North East Inner City's late engagement with YEPP, it scored well on nine of the criteria.

How far the principal features of YEPP's research structure were implemented

Table 4.2 gives an indication of the extent to which each of the Local Programme Sites involved in YEPP adhered to YEPP's research structure. The table shows that Tuzla-Simin Han, Mirafiori, Kristinestad and Parella implemented all of the key features of having a local coordinator, a local researcher, a Local Support Group and of implementing cycles of change. In this analysis, the well-implemented sites and Parella have '+' signs in all of these areas. Antwerp North and Mannheim Neckarstadt-West had no Local Support Group compatible with YEPP requirements, and neither Antwerp North nor Mannheim Neckarstadt-West nor Dublin North East Inner City managed to implement any cycles of change. In the case of Dublin North East Inner City this was because the first action plan was presented after the end of YEPP I.

Table 4.2: The extent to which YEPP's working structure was implemented at each programme site, 2001–06

	Well-implemented sites			Partly implemented sites			Newcomer
	Tuzla-Simin Han	Turin-Mirafiori	Kristine-stad	Turin-Parella	Antwerp North	Mannheim Neckar-stadt-West	Dublin North East Inner City*
Local coordinator	++	++	++	++	++	++	++
Local researcher	++	++	+	++	+	++	+
Local Support Group	++	++	++	++	x	x	++
Cycles of change implemented	++	++	++	++	x	x	x

Notes: Dublin North East Inner City* = 2004 –06; ++ = fully implemented; + = partly implemented; x = not implemented.

Youth and community empowerment

Table 4.3 is more complex and summarises the outcomes for youth and community empowerment. The table shows that the well–implemented sites produced more outcomes and that these outcomes were more substantial. For example, in the area of youth empowerment, in Tuzla-Simin Han and Mirafiori special needs students were involved, while in the partly implemented sites they were not. There was more involvement of youth in the decision making in the well–implemented sites.

For community empowerment, the Local Support Groups were influential in the well–implemented sites, while in the partly implemented sites they were not. In the well–implemented sites there was a greater marshalling of community actors towards 'big' projects aimed at involving the community more fully and holistically. In the partly implemented sites there tended to be 'one-off' activities. In Antwerp North the asset-based community development with RISO was a training programme with unclear outcomes for YEPP, and in Mannheim Neckarstadt-West the impact of YEPP on the neighbourhood management work was not strong.

Table 4.3: The main outcomes of youth and community empowerment for the Local Programme Sites

	Site	Youth empowerment	Community empowerment
YEPP well-implemented	Tuzla-Simin Han	Numbers of youth involved increased sharply; Youth Council; Youth Bank Increased self-confidence Increased engagement in Simin Han and Tuzla New skills learned: leadership training, work training Special-needs students included EmpowerMediaNetwork	The Agora community centre engages citizens to achieve political goals; 'Kooperativa' Local Support Group and community foundation are central Quality of education improving Open centres for youth Community TV
	Turin-Mirafiori	Youth involved in all projects Girls' involvement given priority in later action plan MiraYEPP incubator for small businesses Inclusion of special-needs and mentally ill students EmpowerMediaNetwork	Mirafiori TV boosts image of Mirafiori; movies made Local community organizations involved with YEPP and changed via evaluations Local Support Group developed Community foundation
	Kristinestad	Active citizenship encouraged Youth Council joins Local Support Group Engagement in local politics Transnational Learning and capacity building; health and lifestyle Youth empowerment manifesto adopted by municipal council	Local Support Group influence on municipality Cultural cafe Bi-lingual newspaper Little parliament Youth Council links with Finnish schools TV channel

Table 4.3: continued

	Site	Youth empowerment	Community empowerment
YEPP partly implemented	Turin-Parella	Young people involved in activities Preparation of project proposal for Italian government	Newspaper Folk dancing workshop and activities in gym Street parties
	Antwerp North	Community TV via EmpowerMediaNetwork Transnational youth workshop	Vocational School Asset-based community development with public sector community development office (RISO) Sailing boat project (Hoger Wal) New kids' centre
	Mannheim Neckarstadt-West	Language training via Backpack/Reading Shop Learning responsibility through the arts Campus 'Aktiv' ProFijunior Youth culture and media work	Influence on neighbourhood management and continued involvement Reading Shop Community art and Art Shop in place ProFi lease office
Newcomer	Dublin North East Inner City*	More youth in Young People at Risk programme Youth Forum EmpowerMediaNetwork	Strategic plan for YPAR Integrating foreign nationals Cultural events – EmpowerMediaNetwork, community TV

Note: Dublin North East Inner City* = 2004 –06.

Table 4.4: The main outcomes for the Local Programme Sites of the various partnerships formed

	Site	Partnerships
YEPP well-implemented	Tuzla-Simin Han	Freudenberg and C.S. Mott Foundations especially supportive. Many other foundations also supportive of particular themes and cooperate with each other to achieve common goals Public sector involvement increased over time, especially schools. Also cooperation between schools and business, and with training in ecology Has initiated actions in wider context of Tuzla Private sector involvement has grown
	Turin-Mirafiori	Compagnia di San Paulo Skill building supported, for example, public/private cooperation for incubator Community foundation created Public organization became more and more autonomous with involvement with YEPP Some involvement of high school Social services keep in touch Public library made available YEPP accepted to represent Mirafiori rather than individual groups At end an enterprise joins Local Support Group
	Kristinestad	Swedish cultural foundation Village music community school Youth Council consulted in budget plan Local council accepts YEPP as partner A village council joins YEPP project Link with Ostrobothnia Kristinestad in national conference on youth empowerment Establishment of Nordic network Link with TV company in Norway
YEPP partly implemented	Turin-Parella	Compagnia di San Paulo Some contact with schools Little contact with district – not consulted about new youth centre Little private sector involvement
	Antwerp North	Evens and Bernheim Foundations Public sector community development office (RISO) supports community foundation Hoger Wal sailing boat project for youth in crisis Scarman Trust Timberland
	Mannheim Neckarstadt-West	Freudenberg Foundation, intercultural centre (IKUBIZ), social-pedagogical project (QUIST) Protestant church Local artists Some cooperation with CITY. ProFijunior Cooperation with University
Newcomer	Dublin North East Inner City*	Irish Youth Foundation Public sector in Local Support Group

Note: Dublin North East Inner City* = 2004–06.

Partnerships

Table 4.4 summarises the extent to which partnerships were developed between the various sectors. As for youth and community empowerment, the partnerships in the well-implemented sites are both broader and deeper, with YEPP becoming much more included in the community development futures, and in the case of Kristinestad there were growing international partnerships with other Nordic countries.

In the partly implemented sites, as for youth and community empowerment outcomes, the partnerships were weak and their nature unclear. The involvement of Timberland, for instance, was for one day per year in one school, and this arrangement has terminated.

Transnational activities

Table 4.5 shows that the well-implemented sites were more involved in the transnational work than were the partially implemented sites. It also shows that when the Local Programme Sites were involved, young people found it especially rewarding. It is clear that the sites learnt from each other, particularly in the area of obtaining knowledge about how to develop independent funding via the establishment of community foundations. Much to the disadvantage of young people, the partially implemented sites were all slow to engage in the transnational work and the EmpowerMediaNetwork.

Sustainability

Table 4.6 breaks down the data on the basis of the sustainability of the sites. The table shows that the well-implemented sites became more autonomous than the partially implemented sites, that is, less dependent on foundations for continuing development. Parella and Mannheim Neckarstadt-West are no longer part of YEPP and in Parella there is no further involvement of the supporting foundation because Parella did not wish to continue.

Table 4.5: Local Programme Sites' involvement in transnational activities

	Site	Transnational activity
YEPP well-implemented	Tuzla-Simin Han	Strong involvement – visits and hosting other sites – participated in all transnational events EmpowerMediaNetwork especially effective, led to community TV project Youth Council established on model of Kristinestad
	Turin-Mirafiori	Transnational work very strong Involvement of youth slow but transformed by EmpowerMediaNetwork Youth gain sense of independence
	Kristinestad	Visits to other sites Workshop on music and citizenship Involvement in EmpowerMediaNetwork and community TV meeting in Turin Young people and local coordinator attend Berlin entrepreneurship workshop Links with Norway Youth see this element as the most important Capacity building Visit by National Youth Commission of South Korea
YEPP partly implemented	Turin-Parella	Youth found meetings personally empowering Some involvement in community TV workshop in Turin
	Antwerp North	Slow start but later good connection via EmpowerMediaNetwork Development of community fund inspired by Tuzla-Simin Han
	Mannheim Neckarstadt-West	Very little involvement – later engagement with EmpowerMediaNetwork, but spasmodic
Newcomer	Dublin North East Inner City*	Strong involvement – visits and hosting other sites Youth found involvement very empowering and built self-confidence and new skills Engagement with community TV also enhanced skills, especially social skills

Note: Dublin North East Inner City* = 2004–06.

Table 4.6: Sustainability across the Local Programme Sites

	Site	Sustainability factors
YEPP well-implemented	Tuzla-Simin Han	Community foundation Youth Bank Community Foundation Tuzla
	Turin-Mirafiori	Preparation of the community foundation (officially established 2008)
	Kristinestad	Conference on Education, Democracy and Influence Newspaper Youth Council has bigger role More engagement with municipal council Little Parliament strengthened
YEPP partly implemented	Turin-Parella	Not continued
	Antwerp North	Evens Foundation committed Involvement of the public sector through the Community Development Office, RISO Development of a community fund
	Mannheim Neckarstadt-West	Continued commitment of the Freudenberg Foundation Implementation of neighbourhood management Reading and Art Shops should be made permanent
Newcomer	Dublin North East Inner City*	Continued funding from foundations and statutory agencies Young People at Risk (YPAR) programme is key

Note: Dublin North East Inner City* = 2004–06.

Impact on public policy

Table 4.7 shows the impact of the sites on public policy. In Tuzla and Kristinestad, YEPP's work has led notably to changes in national laws and policies: in Tuzla, around the creation of community foundations; and in Kristinestad, YEPPs holistic vision has been taken on board in the municipality's budget and economic planning. However, elsewhere there is little evidence that this work had a strong impact on public policy over the period 2002–06, although there may be latent effects.

Table 4.7: Policy impact across the Local Programme Sites

	Site	Policy impact
YEPP well-implemented	Tuzla-Simin Han	Community Foundation Simin Han dependent on a change in public policy and the national law Agora helps municipal policies to become more democratic Community Foundation Tuzla established
	Turin-Mirafiori	Signing of agreement between City of Turin and the Compagnia di San Paulo would not have happened without YEPP. Nevertheless, the impact on youth policy was judged to be minimal Turin was involved in the establishment of the Community Foundation Mirafiori and the acceptance of YEPP and its holistic approach were considered a step forward
	Kristinestad	Considerable impact on municipal policies – YEPP's vision incorporated into new Budget and Economy Plan via Youth Council and agreement to fund relevant projects Local Council Youth Office accepts YEPP as partner
YEPP partly implemented	Turin-Parella	Little impact on public policy
	Antwerp North	Little impact on public policy
	Mannheim Neckarstadt-West	Some impact on the neighbourhood management work, which led to a new 'community assembly' that set up working groups on a number of issues
Newcomer	Dublin North East Inner City*	YEPP's inclusion in the Young People at Risk programme may have accelerated its formal recognition by the Irish prime minister. This was also influenced by the reputation of the partners – especially the OECD

Note: Dublin North East Inner City* = 2004–06.

Five years is a very short time in which to show substantial effects on public policy, especially in countries with complex and expensive social welfare systems. This is an area of future development for YEPP.

A summary of summaries

Chapters Three and Four have summarised the data gathered during the first few years of YEPP around a number of themes that are essential to YEPP and to its principles and method. This section will summarise the summaries.

First, it is clear that some Local Programme Sites implemented YEPP's research structure more fully and effectively than others. And if they did so, they met YEPP's 10 non-negotiable principles more completely than did those where the research structure was only partially implemented.

Second, the fully implemented Local Programme Sites were far more successful in creating broad, systemic changes in a number of important domains central to community growth. Table 4.8 provides a summary of these ipacts.

Table 4.8: Comparison of impacts of well-implemented and partly implemented Local Programme Sites

	Well-implemented	Partly implemented
Youth empowerment	High involvement in substantial projects	Low involvement in weakly supported projects
Community empowerment	Local Support Group had strong influence Projects were substantial	Local support had little influence Projects were weak
Partnership	Well developed, with wide ramifications	Poorly developed
Transnational	High levels of involvement, with impacts on initiatives across the Local Programme Sites	Low levels of involvement
Sustainability	High levels of autonomy for the future	Low levels of autonomy, with some sites ceasing to continue
Impact on public policy	Some impact	Little impact

Table 4.8 shows clearly that in the domains of youth and community empowerment, partnership, transnational work, sustainability and, albeit to a lesser extent, in the case of the impact on public policy, the well-implemented sites showed broader and deeper developments. Furthermore, these changes started to appear quickly and to develop in depth over a short period of time. The data presented in Chapter Three

suggest that the underlying causes of these changes are certainly largely attributable to a Local Support Group's systematically implementing a locally agreed plan, and modifying it in the light of evaluation. If the Local Support Group was absent, as in Antwerp North or Mannheim Neckarstadt-West, or dysfunctional, as in Turin-Parella, then YEPP did not take off.

In addition, it is essential to emphasise the importance of the transnational component. The opportunity for disadvantaged youth from different countries to meet each other in their own communities had a profound impact not only on the youngsters themselves but also on the communities and their horizons.

Further discussion of YEPP I

YEPP I was implemented in seven Local Programme Sites in six countries. Five of these countries are members of the EU; the other was Bosnia and Herzegovina, a country in South Eastern Europe which, according to the World Bank (2010), is a lower middle-income country. It is evident from the descriptions given in the previous chapter that each of the Local Programme Sites was different, even though all of them had serious problems of disadvantage of one sort or another – especially low levels of income and high levels of youth unemployment

YEPP I was a research programme that used the same methodology in each of the six countries involved. The analyses provided in earlier chapters suggest that some Local Programme Sites were better implemented than others, with the degree of funding impacting on the quality of the work. This affected the local coordinators and local researchers, especially in regard to the amount of time that was available for the work, with the result that in the well-implemented sites full funding allowed for the hiring of full-time local coordinators and local researchers for the duration of the work, who were then able to form and maintain the Local Support Groups and implement cycles of change. In doing so, these sites also showed evidence of meeting YEPP's 10 fundamental principles.

But establishing the structure was not enough, for in Turin-Parella the criteria were met but the site did not take off, mainly, it seems, because the dynamics of the Local Support Group were too conflictual for agreement to be reached on significant steps forward. It is worth remembering that Parella was as well supported by the local foundation as Turin-Mirafiori, which was a highly successful site. Thus, the existence of structure and finance can easily be derailed by poor hiring appointments and inter-personal factors as well as by a lack of commitment to change.

It is also true that, of the well-implemented sites, neither Turin-Mirafiori nor Tuzla-Simin Han found implementing the YEPP cycles of change and involving a coordinator (Mirafiori) or a researcher (Simin Han) easy to initiate. In both sites there were false starts, but in both sites the local actors could see the potential benefits and worked through the difficulties in order to seek solutions, with the result that both of these sites flourished.

In contrast, in two of the partly implemented sites, Antwerp North and Mannheim Neckarstadt-West, there were continuing problems of initiating cycles of change and using the local researcher to feed back key information about initiatives. But here, more profound difficulties around involving youth in decision making and the commitment of the local foundations to the YEPP model inhibited developments, with the result that in these sites, as well as in Parella, there was less enthusiasm for YEPP, leading to inherent difficulties and ultimately less interest in creating sustainability. Two of these Local Programme Sites, Mannheim Neckarstadt-West and Turin-Parella did not continue. Antwerp North survived because of the commitment of the foundation involved and the appointment of a more dynamic local coordinator.

In all human endeavours, the personalities of the individuals in leadership roles are crucial, and this is also true for YEPP. This means that, in order to implement YEPP successfully, the choice of the coordinator is paramount, especially in maintaining a well-functioning Local Support Group that can work collectively to meet agreed goals and objectively evaluate progress towards meeting them. This observation fits well with the principles of well-run businesses as described by Senge (1990) as 'learning organisations'. Learning organisations facilitate the learning of their members and continuously transform themselves and develop as a result of the business pressures facing them, so as to enable them to remain competitive in the business environment. They have five main features: systems thinking, that is, looking at the organisation as a whole as well as its constituent parts; a commitment to personal learning (personal mastery); a willingness to develop new 'mental models' by having their current views challenged; shared vision to create a common identity and purpose and to motivate people to learn; and team learning to develop shared solutions and problem-solving skills.

The analyses presented also make it clear that the transnational component of YEPP was extremely popular with the young people who became involved and with the local coordinators. It also provided a great vehicle for capacity building. Involvement in transnational work, for example via the EmpowerMediaNetwork, discriminated between the well and partly implemented sites. In all of the well-implemented sites – Tuzla-Simin Han, Turin-Mirafiori, Kristinestad, and including Dublin North East Inner City – there was great enthusiasm for the transnational work. By contrast, in the other sites, Turin-Parella, Antwerp North and Mannheim Neckarstadt-West – this was not the case, certainly for the first few years of YEPP I. The impact of the EmpowerMediaNetwork was extremely motivating, and learning about youth banks and community foundations through the YEPP transnational meetings was crucial in creating the sustainability of YEPP in the Local Programme Sites.

The methodology used

The research and development method used during YEPP I was very focused. It was an action research model that created a Local Support Group to be animated by a local coordinator, with a local researcher serving, among other things, as a critical friend. A programme team in Berlin served to support the implementation of YEPP and to coordinate the internal evaluation in a consistent way across all of the Local Programme Sites. Data were gathered regularly by a number of different means. The data were mainly qualitative and were collected using the CIPP method across mandating, strategic, operational and field levels of the system in the independent, public and private sectors. Furthermore, measurements were repeated across a three-year time period, leading to a complex research design that allowed for comparison between sites on key issues such as youth and community empowerment and partnerships. Even though the research element was side-lined in some sites and the role of the researcher was often not well understood, the evaluations of the actions carried out by the researchers were much appreciated.

However, many of the Local Programme Sites would have welcomed a less demanding evaluation design. Nevertheless, the strength of the model adopted was that it provided good data and it was, as a result, possible to draw strong, generalisable, evidence-based conclusions across the different sites in an international framework.

These data had a strong impact on the design of YEPP II, which, while stressing development and advocacy rather than research, still recognised the importance of evaluation, which remains essential to the YEPP model and capacity building. However, Local Programme Sites varied in their capabilities in regard to developing an evaluation culture, some still finding it difficult to use evaluation to create change, despite strong support from the programme team in Berlin and the development of YEPP manuals.

So does YEPP work – does it cause change?

Does YEPP work? There is no need to equivocate. If YEPP is well implemented, then it works. There is plenty of evidence to indicate that lasting changes took place in these communities. Whether YEPP 'caused' these changes or not is another question that requires further discussion.

Can YEPP be said to have caused change? An important question, raised especially by partnering foundations, was how to know that it was YEPP that 'caused' any observed changes in these communities. It is not possible to throw any light on this issue without evidence, and YEPP was designed to gather data over the duration of its implementation in order to illuminate this question. Furthermore, via the internal and external evaluations these data were gathered from very different sources, thus providing the greatest possibility of recording relevant information. Additionally, data from the internal evaluation was validated by those from the external evaluation. Data were also gathered over time, giving them reliability. It is therefore fair to conclude that the data gathered during the course of YEPP I meet scientific criteria of being both valid and reliable. The data are also 'authentic', since they were gathered from the reality on the ground.

From a scientific point of view, notions of causality tend to be rather restricted to experimental designs using random control groups. Clearly, in a study such as YEPP it is not possible to achieve this 'gold standard' and the best that can be done is to try to link the decisions and actions on the ground with outcomes. The action research-based cycle-of-change model with regular monitoring serving as formative evaluation was the methodology used to achieve this. The approach resembles single-case experimental designs intended to identify causal links between cyclical manipulations of independent variables and corresponding changes in performance levels observed in the dependent variables (Robson, 2011).

Hence, in YEPP's method and evaluation, the importance given to the cycles of change, and the reason why they receive such close attention in the reports described in Chapter Three. In those Local Programme Sites where this approach was well implemented there is clear evidence that decisions taken by the Local Support Group were followed by actions on the ground and that these were modified in the light of the evaluations made, which led in turn to new decisions and new actions, and so on. This pattern could be seen in the well-implemented Local Programme Sites over a number of iterations of the cycle, thus providing evidence that this approach caused the changes observed.

The strength of this model is that it allows strong conclusions to be drawn. By contrast, in the partly implemented sites the cycles of change were not implemented and therefore there is no basis on which to make such conclusions. However, there were changes in these Local Programme Sites that probably came about through the general engagement in a programme with other foundations and through additional funding. In the light of these difficulties, a different approach to the causal question is called for.

One such approach to answering the 'Did YEPP cause change?' question can be taken from the work on counterfactual theory (Lewis, 1973). An analysis along these lines would focus on whether or not change would have taken place if, in this case, YEPP had not existed. This is perhaps a more sympathetic line of enquiry for projects as complex as YEPP, and causal interpretations can still be made even if the more rigorous cycle-of-change method has not been fully implemented, as was the case in some of the YEPP Local Programme Sites.

For instance, the transnational work would not have taken place without YEPP and therefore YEPP can claim to have caused the outcomes related to the transnational work. It is extremely unlikely to have happened by chance. Thus, YEPP caused the EmpowerMediaNetwork to happen, and since this was one of the very strong outcomes of YEPP, engaging many young people and with lasting effects in most sites, this must be seen as a major benefit. Similar arguments can be applied to other outcomes of the transnational work such, as the generalised interest in the 'Youth Bank' and the creation of Community Foundations. Engagement in these activities emerged even in the partly implemented sites – albeit rather weakly.

While the result of the transnational element of the YEPP work is clear, it is much more difficult to disentangle the variables linked to the changes that took place locally in the Local Programme Sites if the cycle-of-change approach was not used. Since changes did occur even in Local Programme Sites with a partially implemented YEPP model, it becomes arguable that the YEPP cycle-of-change approach is not a necessary condition for change. Thus, any organised approach that demands additional staff time and gathering of data via a monitoring process and that provides assistance by a professional transnational team will work to some degree. But the key question is: *will it work as efficiently?*

Certainly those Local Programme Sites that implemented a full YEPP model were more successful than those that did not. In those that did not, there are a range of reasons. Hostility in Antwerp North (finally overcome); the bureaucratic complexity of the system in which YEPP was embedded in Dublin North East Inner City (finally resolved); a lack of commitment to the model by the relevant foundation in Mannheim Neckarstadt-West (not resolved); and apathy and internal tensions in Turin-Parella (unresolved, through no fault of the supporting foundation – see Turin-Mirafiori as a contrast).

This discussion reveals the complexities involved in carrying out research and development work of this sort and the need for persistence and flexibility. Data serving as evidence of success or failure is crucial in making investment decisions and programme choices. For YEPP, on-going involvement during the course of the work allowed for corrections to be made on the basis of reliable and valid information either on the ground or at the level of foundation involvement in the steering committee. These features of YEPP have allowed it endure over a 10-year period and expand to new sites, and to have a long-term future in making an important contribution to tackling the social exclusion of young people at risk. This outcome alone has to be testament to the overall success of YEPP. YEPP II and the planned future of YEPP are discussed in the following chapters.

FIVE

YEPP II: learning from YEPP I

YEPP II: 2007–11

The internal and external evaluations of YEPP I provided convincing evidence that YEPP works in fully implemented and supported sites. In addition, following consultations with partner organisations and key actors of the YEPP network and with the foundations that had expressed an interest in participating in the next phase of YEPP, the partners and stakeholders of YEPP decided to extend the programme by a further multi-year period (2007–11). This decision reflected the understanding that bringing about sustainable social change in disadvantaged areas through an empowerment and partnership approach is a long-term process to which they were willing to commit.

Furthermore they had come to recognise the growing need for a holistic, multi-level programme such as YEPP, and this understanding led the partners to decide not only to continue working in the existing programme sites of YEPP I but also to expand to other disadvantaged communities. This decision also had a strategic purpose. The partners and stakeholders wanted to establish a critical number of sites in order to give extra weight to their efforts to influence policies at different levels. In order to achieve this ambition they decided to shift the focus of the programme from research and development to one emphasising development, dissemination and advocacy. The importance of evaluation was recognised, but it was decided to stress self-evaluation as an integral part of the work.[1]

Strategies for YEPP II in response to lessons learnt

In the process of designing the second phase of YEPP, specific strategies were developed in order to reflect the lessons learnt from the first phase, as presented in the previous chapters, and to overcome remaining challenges. In the following sections, different examples of lessons learnt – which are obviously interlinked with each other – and how they were used in creating YEPP II are described.

Lesson 1: YEPP works and it works best when fully implemented

The evaluation of the first phase of YEPP had shown that three factors were crucial for a successful implementation of YEPP and to bring about change:

- needs of the community for change and strong motivation and commitment of local stakeholders to bring about change;
- clear understanding of and commitment to the common ground across all the Local Programme Sites: that is, the YEPP principles, the overall programme goals and the concept of change;
- reliable support and resources.

Since the second phase was about to expand YEPP to other disadvantaged communities, these factors needed to be taken into consideration in the new programme sites. The following strategies were developed, based on the lessons learnt from YEPP I.

Common ground

The common ground on which the stakeholders worked in YEPP II were:

- the 10 non-negotiable features of YEPP I, which were confirmed;
- the three overall programme goals; and
- the concept of change.

YEPP's mission is to develop a sustainable, participatory planning process, creating an active civil society involving disadvantaged children and youth across Europe. To accomplish this mission, YEPP pursues three goals:

1. Youth and community empowerment
   To enable disadvantaged children and youth to take control of their lives and to contribute to their local communities as equals alongside community leaders so that they become active citizens of Europe and their national societies; to embed youth empowerment in community empowerment, which promotes changes to the environment in which children and youth grow up.

2. Partnerships

To form strong and sustainable cross-sectoral partnerships and strategic alliances, at local, national and transnational levels in order to foster youth and community empowerment.

3. Advocacy

To influence public policy so that the principles of youth empowerment, community empowerment and partnership become mainstreamed in public and independent sector programmes across Europe.

In YEPP II, acceptance of these goals was formalised with each partner through the signing of a Memorandum of Understanding committing them to the common ground. And, in so doing, the YEPP stakeholders decided that YEPP II should focus on advocating for policies in support of youth and community empowerment, social inclusion and active citizenship of young people living in disadvantaged communities in Europe. Influencing policies and mainstreaming the YEPP policy messages would become the crucial goals and would absorb the available expertise and funding.[2]

Selection of programme sites

The selection of new Local Programme Sites was carried out in a more structured and thorough way than in YEPP I. 'Criteria for Including New Programme Sites and Affiliates' were established and communicated with interested stakeholders. For a new programme site, the criteria included the definition of a YEPP programme site and characteristics of the area, the joint vision, necessary funding arrangements and a defined local infrastructure with a Local Support Group, a local coordinator and evaluation facilitator and their respective tasks. A project or local initiative could become a YEPP affiliate site if it followed a compatible concept of change and shared a common interest in strategic collaboration. The document also included 'YEPP's Assumptions about Change' and 'The Guiding Principles of YEPP's Concept of Change'.

Furthermore, the key partners in each new YEPP programme site had to sign a Memorandum of Understanding committing to the vision, overall programme goals and inclusion criteria, as well as to establishing the YEPP advisory infrastructure, including the Local Support Group, a local coordinator and an evaluation facilitator.

Capacity building and support

Reflecting the lessons learnt from YEPP I, more attention was given to capacity building, support and technical assistance for the local teams and the young people. Peer learning became an important technique for capacity building and the local teams of the programme sites of Phase I became consultants to the new local teams. These sites became known as 'consultation sites'.

Practitioners' Handbook

As a result of Phase I, the first edition of the *YEPP Practitioners' Handbook — Youth and Community Empowerment in Practice* was published (Bleckmann et al, 2007) as a practical guide for the local teams in implementing the concept of change and, in particular, the YEPP cycle of change. The content of this handbook reflected the wealth of experiences from the seven programme sites of YEPP I. All of the experiences and results from the internal and external evaluations were taken into account in the handbook, which contained the essence of the concept and the experiences of YEPP at the local level. Practitioners were guided through the YEPP cycle of change. It also outlined the benefits of cross-border networking and learning at national and international levels.

The *Practitioners' Handbook* complemented the technical assistance provided by members of the programme team during their regular site visits. The local teams worked with the handbook for about a year and gave their feedback to the programme team, with the result that a second edition was published (Krüger et al, 2009).

The online International Resource Centre for Youth and Community Empowerment

The International Resource Centre for Youth and Community Empowerment (IRC) was established so as to provide an online platform for the partners of YEPP to pool their expertise and resources in order to create a strong central support structure for all aspects and levels of the programme. Furthermore, through the IRC, the partners had an opportunity to identify, explore and make known other innovative approaches and examples of best practice. As well as supporting the local actors in developing action plans, evaluating the progress made and learning from a variety of local, national and international case studies, the IRC reinforced the shifting focus of the programme towards public advocacy, expansion of the network and influencing policies. The IRC also contributed to YEPP's communication and public relations strategies, connecting YEPP with new partners and providing these with information, and developing policy messages and strategic plans at various levels. For example, the IRC published the handbooks and manuals in order to support the implementation of the concept of change, including the monitoring and evaluation design.

Training

Training was organised and follow-up coaching provided by the YEPP Programme Team at workshops and conferences and during site visits. One such example was the Youth Bank training, which took place in August 2009. Following the training, local Youth Banks (Box 5.1) were set up in five programme sites. A transnational Youth Bank was established that gave a major grant to a transnational music festival run by young people. A large group of youth participants from five Local Programme Sites as well as the local community attended the festival.

Box 5.1: Youth Bank

Youth Bank is an innovative grant-making initiative run by young people for young people. Local Youth Banks provide small grants to projects led by young people that benefit the community and the young people taking part. Youth Bank is unique in that it is the young people themselves who make decisions about how local Youth Banks are managed and run. They make joint decisions about real money used in real-life situations. Youth Bank is a strong youth empowerment tool for young people living in disadvantaged areas. Both groups of young people benefit: the Youth Bank committee comprised solely of young people, and those young people who submit proposals and implement their projects if they are awarded a grant.

Another example was the transnational advocacy training, a training of trainers which took place in November 2009. The objectives of the training were that participants should develop a deeper understanding of advocacy work and its main elements, become familiar with a set of tools for developing and implementing an advocacy strategy and have practised using them.

Lesson 2: Difficulties in implementing the research design

YEPP I was conceived as a research project with a strong evaluation component. While this element proved difficult to implement, its value was also appreciated. As noted, YEPP II is a development project and wanted to continue to build an evaluation culture in the Local Programme Sites while at the same time avoiding the costs and complexities of an external evaluation. The evaluation design was therefore reviewed and the following strategies were developed in response to this particular lesson learnt.

Participatory YEPP Monitoring and Evaluation Design (PYME)

Because evaluation is an integral part of the YEPP concept of change, and in particular with regard to the cycle of change (Figure 3), the evaluation design for YEPP II was refocused and more closely linked with the concept of change, thus involving people from the Local Programme Sites in the evaluation process. Accordingly, the evaluation design for YEPP Phase II intended to increase the active participation of the local teams in the evaluation process and embedded self-evaluation more deeply in the daily routine of YEPP participants at the local level. This was also considered to be an important tool to support youth and community empowerment and to further strengthen an evaluation culture. Furthermore, this was seen as a capacity-building strategy with the potential to be of benefit to the local actors also, beyond YEPP. To assist in this process, it was agreed that each Local Programme Site should appoint an evaluation facilitator who would help the programme participants to carry out the evaluation.

Figure 3: Linking the concept of change with the PYME design

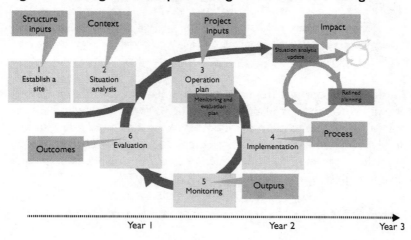

As YEPP continued to work at different levels (local, regional/national and transnational within Europe) this multi-level structure of YEPP had important implications for its evaluation. YEPP's overall programme goals and objectives are valid at all levels of the YEPP structure and their attainment, and therefore need to be evaluated both across all levels (that is, for the programme as a whole) and for each level separately.

The Evaluation Design and Implementation Plan for YEPP II were developed in a jointly facilitated process by members of the steering committee, an experienced local researcher of YEPP I who had worked in Turin-Mirafiori, the two Programme Officers of the YEPP Programme Team, the two authors of this report, Peter Evans and Angelika Krüger, and a consultation process at local level, and were introduced and agreed in May 2008 (Krüger et al, 2008). They were based on the reconfirmation of the three overall goals of YEPP II – youth and community empowerment, partnership and advocacy. The evaluation design of YEPP I and the experience of the internal and external evaluation processes were taken into consideration. The design was inspired by other concepts, such as the Logic Model (McCawley, undated).

As noted, the decision was made not to have an external evaluation, but to focus instead on enabling the YEPP stakeholders at local and transnational level to meet the purposes of the evaluation, that is, to learn from experience, to assess outcomes, and to develop advocacy. The resulting evaluation reports are still required and should give sound, evidence-based information about how to create positive change for and with young people and the communities they live in, allowing this information to be disseminated and used to influence public opinion, policies and political decision making and accountability.

Finally, the specific concept of the PYME approach was developed and agreed. It is participatory because local monitoring teams carry out the monitoring and provide continuous feedback to the local stakeholders. They are supported by an evaluation facilitator and the YEPP Programme Team. Monitoring is defined as the continuous assessment of short-term changes that refer to objectives at the different levels –local, regional, national and transnational. Evaluation is the assessment of medium- and long-term changes referring to the achievements of YEPP's overall programme goals. The PYME design defines what to monitor and evaluate and how to do it. In other words, the PYME design gives answers to three fundamental questions:

- How can we assess change?
- What changes do we want to assess?

• What tells us if such changes have occurred, and to what extent?

Based on the same design, the programme team, in cooperation with the local teams, monitors and evaluates the transnational activities.

Manual for Evaluation Facilitators and Manual for Monitoring Teams

In October 2008, the first edition of the *Manual for Evaluation Facilitators, Part 1: Guidelines and Part 2: Toolbox* was published (Strocka et al, 2008). The manual is a practical guide for the monitoring and evaluation process in YEPP Local Programme Sites. It puts the Evaluation Design and Implementation Plan for YEPP II into practice. After a year of working with the manual, a second edition was published (Strocka et al, 2009).

At the same time, and in two editions, the *Manual for Monitoring Teams on Participatory Output Monitoring* (POM) (Engelhardt-Wendt et al, 2008 and 2009) was published, which is a practical guide for the teams in the Local Programme Sites. It provides a hands-on explanation of the method of POM which is part of the PYME.

Capacity building

In order to support the implementation of the monitoring and evaluation process as an integral part of the cycle of change, training for all evaluation facilitators and local coordinators took place in November 2008. This was followed by on-site coaching and further training for newly appointed evaluation facilitators, and transnational reflection meetings in the course of the second phase of YEPP.

Lesson 3: Partnerships – the need for different approaches to public and private sector involvement

YEPP originated as a collaborative project of foundations, and their partnership has remained the bedrock of the programme during YEPP II and it was confirmed that YEPP II would remain a foundation-led programme until the end of the second phase. Yet, YEPP's strength has been the partnership of foundations with other partners who contribute their expertise and networks to the programme. In the second phase, building new partnerships with foundations as well as strengthening cross-sectoral partnerships with public and private sectors is seen as being crucial for achieving the overall programme goals.

Involvement of the public sector

Taking the lessons learnt from YEPP I into consideration, more attention was given to the involvement of the public sector. In the case of new programme sites, it was a precondition that the municipalities should have a stake in selecting them and take on board certain responsibilities. For example, in the new Italian programme sites, several municipalities provided the staff time of the local coordinators and evaluation facilitators. Together with the other partners, they co-signed the Memorandum of Understanding. In several municipalities, the YEPP concept was utilised for designing their own youth policies and this helped considerably to mainstream YEPP results.[3]

Involvement of the private sector

Although many attempts were made to involve businesses (small and large) in the YEPP work at local and transnational level, following the recommendation to involve them from the very beginning and to develop elements of YEPP together, YEPP did not succeed in involving partners from the private sector. This part of the cross-sectoral partnership did not work well, except for a few local examples, such as in Tuzla–Simin Han (Bosnia and Herzegovina), where the Local Programme Site initiated a programme of job-experience schemes with local employers.

Lesson 4: Successful work at transnational level, but not all sites seeing its value

As the multi-level approach of integrated work with young people and other stakeholders at local, regional, national and transnational levels was one of the key conceptual elements of YEPP I, it was further developed and strengthened in YEPP II towards bringing about tangible and measurable results. The focus shifted towards advocacy, and for utilised this purpose the combination of the empowerment of children and youth in their communities with the political influence of a transnational network.

The transnational dimension interlinked with the local/regional/national dimension, in particular, was one of the success stories of YEPP I, although not all sites were fully on board. In YEPP II, the strategy for overcoming this problem was to design the activities at transnational level so as to meet the needs of the young people and the local teams in a more meaningful way, keeping the inspirational and motivational character of the events. More outreach work was done to bring all the local stakeholders on board and each event was thoroughly evaluated in order to improve the work. More attention was given to the meaningful interlinking with the local level. On the one hand, all stakeholders were involved in preparing for the transnational events with local projects and tasks and, on the other, local activities followed up the transnational event in order to achieve the next level of development.

Each year at least one major transnational event took place, which was usually organised in cooperation with the local team of one of the programme sites or in Berlin, where the programme office was located. A considerable number of these events were capacity-building workshops and training for young people as well as for local coordinators and evaluation facilitators addressing issues such as advocacy strategies, Youth Bank, media (create and share), fundraising and so on.

The YEPP community grew during the course of YEPP II and, as of May 2011 (see Preface, Figure 1), has become a platform for a network of 18 Local Programme Sites in eight European countries. As activities of the YEPP community network, community conferences and youth meetings took place in Dublin 2008, Genoa 2010 and Görlitz/Zgorzelec (Germany/Poland) 2011. These conferences and youth meetings were theme based and increasingly oriented towards advocacy.

The overall theme of the conference and youth meeting in Dublin 2008 was 'Leading the Way – Another Europe is Possible! Changing Policies through Youth and Community Empowerment and Partnerships.'

In Genoa 2010, the overall theme was 'Be the Change! Listening to Youth Voices – Learning from Community Actions', and the Youth Meeting on advocacy addressed the issues 'Diversity, Dialogue and Inclusion – European Youth as Agents of Social Change'. At this meeting young people met local politicians to discuss youth participation in decision making processes and developed 'golden rules' of youth participation.

In Görlitz/Zgorzelec 2011, the overall theme was 'YEPP: 10 Years of Change' and the Youth Meeting addressed the issues 'Building Structures, Creating Pathways towards Sustainable Youth Participation', and thus continued to address the orientation towards advocacy. Together with local politicians from five different countries, young people discussed youth participation in decision-making processes and the creation of appropriate structures and channels.

The joint project of YEPP, the EmpowerMediaNetwork, became even more important during YEPP II. Experiences during the first phase had shown that media work with disadvantaged young people was a strong empowerment tool and had supported them to make their voices heard. It was utilised by the young people for their advocacy work. Ultimately, EmpowerMediaNetwork has been helping young people from all walks of life discover their ability to shape and create their own futures.

Advocacy work was started at the European level. In cooperation with the local teams, in particular the young people, with the steering committee and partners, the programme team developed strategies for dissemination and advocacy at all levels, and in particular at the European level. Important contacts were established with the Directorate-General for Education and Culture of the European Commission of the European Union, in particular the Youth in Action Programme. The results of the evaluations of the Youth in Action Programme and YEPP I were shared and possible cooperation was explored further.

As a result of the lessons learnt with regard to the need for more structured and focused capacity building and the transnational dimension, the YEPP support structures facilitating learning opportunities were significantly strengthened. The YEPP Programme Team, in cooperation with external consultants and members of the steering committee, acted as a transnational support agency facilitating capacity building and transfer of know-how at all levels; providing technical assistance and compiling handbooks such as the *Practitioners' Handbook* and manuals such as the *Manual for Evaluation Facilitators and Monitoring Teams* as practical guides on how to implement the concept of change and the participatory YEPP monitoring and evaluation design; facilitating exchanges and learning opportunities at transnational events such as conferences, workshops and training, youth exchanges, joint projects; and carrying out the overall evaluation of the programme. The online YEPP International Resource Centre for Youth and Community Empowerment (IRC) was established, which is one of the tools of the support structure and is managed by the programme team. It provides an online platform through which the partners of YEPP pool their expertise and resources in order to create a strong central support structure for all aspects and levels of the programme. Furthermore, through the IRC, the partners identify, explore and make known other innovative approaches and examples of best practice.

Lesson 5: Sustainability needs to be a focus

From the very beginning of YEPP there was a strategy to sustain strategic planning processes, active citizenship, and the infrastructure to bring about sustainable change beyond the programme phases. Different measures were taken in YEPP II so as to ensure that more attention would be given to sustainability.

- At the local level, youth participation in decision-making processes was further strengthened. Youth participation in the Local Support Groups became a priority in most of the programme sites. In some of the new sites, the Local Support Groups were formed solely by young people and youth organisations.
- Strengthening cross-sectoral partnership and building strategic alliances for impacting on policies has become another priority.
- The cooperation with local governments for influencing youth policies, mainstreaming innovations and coordinating service delivery have been further developed and strengthened.

Turning the informal Local Support Groups into formal structures, following the model of the Community Foundation Tuzla, was further discussed and promoted. The Community Foundation Mirafiori (Turin, Italy) was established with the Local Support Group, which had been transformed into a non-for-profit association, as one of the founders.

One of the support measures was capacity building. For example, youth participation in decision-making processes was promoted through training on the Youth Bank approach. (See Lesson 1 above.)

Lesson 6: Impact on policies

Impacting on policies was a major strategy for sustaining the achievements and examples of best practices of YEPP. Although this was on the agenda of YEPP from the very beginning, the evaluation showed that not much had been achieved during YEPP I, mainly because it had been decided to go into depth in a limited number of sites in order to learn what works and what does not work and to create a quality concept for social change. This work took the whole time-span of the first phase and it was too early to take the important step of impacting on policies.

As noted above in Lesson 5, mainstreaming innovations is a key factor that can only be achieved through influencing policies at the level where the decision-making processes take place. This may be the case at local, regional and/or national levels.

When the decision was made to prolong YEPP for another multi-year period, the stakeholders felt more comfortable with focusing, in a more substantial way, on advocacy and, as a result, this became the explicit third goal of YEPP II. YEPP II pursued the goal of influencing public policy so that the principles of youth empowerment, community empowerment and partnership could become mainstreamed in public and independent programmes across Europe. The following strategies were developed in response to this particular lesson.

Expansion

The partners in YEPP recognised that the collective efforts to influence policies in support of disadvantaged children and youth and the communities they live in could be greatly strengthened by building a critical mass of Local Programme Sites, as well as by joining forces with more stakeholders and partners at the different levels. More effective and sustainable changes could be achieved by building strategic alliances with more local, regional and national stakeholders, governments and administrations, foundations, NGOs and businesses across Europe, as well as with the European Commission.

Based on the experiences of YEPP I, sets of criteria for the inclusion of new partners and programme sites were developed. New collaborations were confirmed by signing a Memorandum of Understanding, and different approaches to expansion were put into action and new foundation partners joined.

- In 2007, a successful application for YEPP II kept the Ford Foundation (US) on board and the representative of the foundation stayed on the steering committee until the end of the grant period.
- In 2008, the Barrow Cadbury Trust (UK) joined YEPP as a full partner and member of the YEPP steering committee for a three-year period to 2011. The intention was to support a YEPP programme site in Birmingham (UK) but, due to local problems, the possible local partners decided against joining YEPP.
- In the same year, Atlantic Philanthropies (Ireland) awarded a grant to YEPP in support of the 3rd YEPP Community Conference and Youth Meeting, which took place in Dublin in 2008. However, it did not become a full partner.

From March 2011 to January 2012 (when the steering committee was dissolved), the partner foundations of YEPP and members of the steering committee were: Barrow Cadbury Trust (UK), Charles Stewart Mott Foundation (US) (vice chair), Compagnia di San Paolo (Italy) (chair), Evens Foundation (Belgium), Foundation Bernheim (Belgium) and Irish Youth Foundation (Ireland).

Foundations that were, or still are involved in YEPP programme sites are: Compagnia di San Paolo (all Italian sites), Evens Foundation (Antwerp North, Belgium and Warszawa Bielany, Poland), ERSTE Stiftung (Austria) (Košice, Slovakia), Fondazione Cassa di Risparmio della Spezia (La Spezia, Italy), Fondazione Cassa di Risparmio di Cuneo (Langhe, Italy), Community Foundation Savonese (Albenga and Loano, Italy), Freudenberg Stiftung (Germany) and Charles Stewart Mott Foundation (Community Foundation Tuzla, Bosnia and Herzegovina), Irish Youth Foundation (Dublin North East Inner City, Ireland), Robert Bosch Stiftung (Germany) (Görlitz/Zgorzelec, Germany/Poland).

New programme sites and affiliate sites

One approach to expansion was to increase the number of programme sites in those countries where a YEPP programme site existed already and to disseminate the YEPP concept of change. Through this so-called 'natural growth' process five new sites were established in Italy (Albenga, Genoa-Cornigliano, La Spezia, Langhe and Loano); two in Finland (Kimitoön and Väståboland); one in Bosnia and Herzegovina (Gornja Tuzla) (as of January 2011).

Another new programme site in Italy, Alassio, came on board at the beginning of 2007 but terminated its work within YEPP in 2010, going its own way in trying to improve the situation of young people in the municipality.

Expanding YEPP II to other countries was either initiated by foundations or prepared by seeking collaboration with other foundations, local governments and NGOs. As of March 2011, three new YEPP programme sites have been added in a 'geographical growth process' in Poland (Warsaw-Bielany and Zgorzelec) and in Germany (Görlitz). The programme site in Warsaw was initiated by the Evens Foundation, which has an operational basis in Warsaw. The new programme site Görlitz (Germany)/Zgorzelec (Poland) was initiated by the programme team and supported by the Robert Bosch Stiftung (Germany), which has an interest in supporting cross-border activities with Eastern and Central European countries.

Major efforts were undertaken to seek further expansion of the programme in Eastern, Central and South-East European countries and former Soviet Union (FSU) countries with the support of a consultant to the programme team. An NGO in Osijek, Croatia, came on board, was introduced to the YEPP approach and trained in PYME and it explored the circumstances of becoming a YEPP programme site, but was forced to withdraw for financial reasons.

A more challenging approach to expanding the programme's scope was to focus on a specific disadvantaged target group – the 'target group growth process'. Promoted by the Austrian foundation, ERSTE Stiftung, a new programme site was established in the Košice region of Slovakia in 2009 with a special focus on Roma inclusion. The programme site encompasses four villages with Roma and non-Roma population. The local team comprises two local coordinators, one Roma and one non-Roma, as well as two evaluation facilitators, one Roma and one non-Roma. They are in the process of building the Local Support Group as well as analysing the situation by identifying the needs, resources and key challenges (that is, the context description).

YEPP also attempted to expand the programme's reach by seeking collaboration with sites that follow a compatible approach to become *affiliate sites* providing learning opportunities and joining in as strategic partners. The Gate project in Turin Porta Palazzo became the first affiliate site of YEPP.

Involvement of local authorities from the outset

In their attempt to establish new programme sites and to influence local and regional policies, the YEPP partners tried to involve the local authorities in the process from the very beginning. Experience had shown that the earlier public authorities become involved, the greater is their commitment. The goal of partnering with the local authorities was to build trust, to share responsibility, to create synergies and joint activities and to win allies for developing sustainable variations of the YEPP approach which reflect local conditions and which have a good chance of being mainstreamed in the future. The YEPP partners promoted the integration of local authorities within the transnational network through focused meetings of local politicians and representatives of administrations, usually at the YEPP Community Conferences and Youth Meetings.

Involving young people in advocacy: capacity building, dialogue and media-supported communication

From 2009, YEPP II promoted the involvement of young people in advocating for what they want to change. This strategy included working on the empowerment of young people to have their voices heard, on building strategic collaboration among young people in the same region, on establishing contacts between young people and decision makers at local, regional, national and European levels, and on creating opportunities for dialogue between young people and politicians.

In 2008, the 3rd YEPP Community Conference and Youth Meeting provided a platform for young people to express their views on 'A Europe with Us and for Us' and to address the challenges, possibilities and actions to make it real.

Capacity building is a crucial strategy for success. In 2009, a transnational advocacy training, to train trainers, took place in Gollwitz, Germany. It was a follow-up from the YEPP Community Conference and Youth Meeting in Dublin, 2008. The objectives of the training were that participants should develop a deeper understanding of advocacy work and its main elements; become familiar with a set of tools for developing and implementing an advocacy strategy and practise using them. They developed ideas and drafted strategies for advocacy projects in their Local Support Groups, especially together with young people, and gained inspiration and practical tools for facilitation of workshops with the young people in their Local Programme Sites. After the training, most of the participants conducted training workshops with young people in order to support them to formulate and convey their policy messages and make their voices heard. As a result, local and regional advocacy actions were discussed and developed together with the local teams and support groups. In Liguria, Italy, for example, a Youth Advocacy Group was established comprising youth delegates from four YEPP programme sites.

In 2010, advocacy became a clear focus of the 4th YEPP Community Conference and Youth Meeting in Genoa, Italy. It sported the title 'Be the Change! Listening to Youth Voices – Learning from Community Actions'. It was attended by young people, youth policy makers and local YEPP teams from 18 YEPP programme sites in eight European countries. A total of about 130 participants, including 49 youth delegates, 32 local coordinators and evaluation facilitators, 15 local politicians and 6 representatives of YEPP partner foundations met to discuss new ways of getting young people involved in their communities and beyond. Youth participation took centre stage at this event.

The Youth Meeting on Advocacy, in particular, focused on 'Diversity, Dialogue and Inclusion – European Youth as Agents of Social Change'. In preparation for this event, young people were encouraged to identify – with the help of their local advocacy trainer or local coordinator – a politician in their town responsible for youth policy whom they wanted to invite to the conference and youth meeting. They needed to establish contact with the person and explain about the upcoming event. In several cases, they met with the politicians to give them more information about their advocacy actions and asked if they would be interested in attending the youth meeting and the conference. This resulted in the participation of 15 local politicians representing Belgium, Bosnia and Herzegovina, Finland, Italy and Poland.

At the transnational meeting, the youth delegates from all Local Programme Sites had the opportunity to exchange their experiences in advocacy with the other participants, discuss their successes and challenges, and reflect upon where they run into problems which only political decisions can remove and find ways for improvement. Furthermore, this meeting gave young people an opportunity to put their advocacy skills into practice, talking directly to local politicians from their own and other countries as well as bringing their issues onto the political agenda.

The youth delegates had prepared a contribution to an interactive exhibition titled 'Images to Influence – Young People's Visions, Voices and Actions', in which they shared what it means to live as a young person in their particular neighbourhood, town, city; what they were able to change and what they still wanted to change. After the conference, delegates had had an opportunity to visit the exhibition; a talk show, titled 'Visions, Voices and Actions – Young People and Politicians in Dialogue', gave youth delegates the opportunity to exchange their local experiences with peers from other countries and to engage in discussions with politicians from various YEPP sites. In the following discussion in country working groups, youth delegates had an opportunity to discuss with their local politician how to strengthen youth participation in decision-making processes in their municipalities.

The Youth Meeting concluded with identifying the 'Golden Rules of Youth Participation in Decision-making Processes' (Box 5.2), which were shared with all conference delegates, followed by presentations by the Youth Bank Committees on their progress and the results of the first calls for proposals from young people for young people and the communities in which they live.

Box 5.2: The Golden Rules of Youth Participation in Decision-making Processes

4th YEPP Community Conference and Youth Meeting, Genoa, 12–14 October 2010

1. Personal attitudes
- Be aware of what you want and how you want to get it
- Be stubborn and persistent
- Be able to compromise
- Be polite
- Be ready to address challenges
- Talk to politicians
- Involve other people who can help you with your projects
- Accept different opinions and personalities

2. Youth representation
- Push for quotas of young people in all political parties
- Promote the involvement of young people in business structures
- Increase youth representation in municipal committees

3. Youth structures
- Set up a Pupils' Council in every school to meet and debate
- Give more weight to Youth Parliaments so that adults listen
- Organise meetings between Youth and City Councils, young people and politicians
- Appoint a Youth Spokesperson to provide consultancy on youth issues
- Establish regional Youth Councils

4. Cooperation with adults
- Strengthen links between school and labour market
- Make young people aware of local support resources
- Give youth a chance to change something in their city and realise their own ideas

- Lower the voting age census to 16
- Need for more interaction

5. Strategy for taking action
  - Identify the problem
  - Work in team, respect other opinions
  - Make petitions to show public support and unity
  - Start with small problems before tackling the big ones

In 2011, the dialogue between young people, local teams and local politicians continued at the YEPP Community Conference and Youth Meeting in Görlitz/Zgorzelec in order to discuss how the voices of young people could be better heard in the future, which organisational structures might be helpful and how to continue the dialogue at local level. It was particularly inspiring and helpful to discuss these issues with two young politicians from Kristinestad who are members of the municipal council and board. They were able to share a number of best practice examples, and their experiences of how to achieve youth participation in policy making proved very helpful for the youth delegates and politicians from other countries.

The capacity-building strategy included media work with young people in the programme sites as well as in transnational media workshops. The EmpowerMediaNetwork, initiated by YEPP, was further strengthened and developed a methodology to explore issues such as identity and active citizenship, the ethical use of media to foster a sense of global solidarity and fight social exclusion, and the threats and opportunities of Web 2.0. In a number of annual transnational workshops, participants developed their creative, social and cultural potential by means of non-formal and informal learning methods. They were empowered and inspired to create and distribute meaningful digital media on issues important to them so that they could have an impact on their communities. The media-supported communication made the voice of young people better heard.

Notes
[1] After a period of reflection on the key successes and the changes YEPP had caused, on the one hand, and the remaining challenges and lessons learnt from the first phase, on the other hand, the partners and key actors of YEPP agreed at the end of 2006 on the YEPP II Programme Plan and Budget 2007 (January)–2011 (June), and in 2008 on the Evaluation Design and Implementation Plan for YEPP Phase II.

[2] This implied that the originally planned second strand of YEPP II – replicating and disseminating the YEPP approach to new contexts outside Europe – was finally abandoned.

[3] The issue was raised whether representatives of the municipalities involved in YEPP should be represented on the steering committee. This proposal was turned down, referring to the decision that YEPP continued as a foundation-led programme. Therefore, the decision making at the transnational level and the overall responsibility for the whole programme stayed with the steering committee, including representatives of the partner foundations, the NEF (providing the legal framework for YEPP) and the INAgGmbH.

SIX

YEPP II: portraits and overall programme outcomes

The first five chapters in this book have introduced YEPP and its logic and, through a systematic evaluation, have argued that there is good evidence that the YEPP model causes desired changes in the disadvantaged communities in which it is working, thereby engaging constructively many of the young people living there. Based on this confidence, foundation investment continued for a further period and Chapter Five describes how YEPP developed from a research programme into a development programme.

This chapter provides brief portraits of some of the YEPP Local Programme Sites in order to provide a better picture of how YEPP works on the ground. Information on the five remaining Local Programme Sites (that formed YEPP I), is updated, and a selection of the new sites that began under YEPP II are presented thematically, in order to indicate YEPP's versatility. The themes are:

• expansion within a country
• cooperation across frontiers
• including Roma young people.

The remaining YEPP I sites

Dublin North East Inner City[1]

Dublin's North East Inner City community has a long history not only of social and economic disadvantage but also of community response based on strong local leadership and the state's involvement as a partner. Community development and advocacy are led by the Inner City Organisation Network (ICON), which represents 65 local community and voluntary organisations. Recently, immigrant communities have arrived and there has been growth in private home ownership.

The Young People at Risk (YPAR) initiative grew out of ICON, and in 2003 this group was brought under the auspices of the Local Child Protection Committee of the Health Service Executive, a statutory body concerned, as its name suggests, with child protection and welfare.

YPAR became the local partner of YEPP 'to have an exchange with like-minded people across Europe; to promote youth participation and to open up opportunities for young people at risk to get involved in transnational activities' (Dolphin, 2011, p 3).

As described in Chapters Three and Four, the YEPP/YPAR collaboration began late in the YEPP I phase and, because of shortage of time was unable to implement cycles of change. However, this changed, and in 2006, following a situational analysis, the first cycle began. The situational analysis confirmed the large number of voluntary and community organisations working in the area, as well as a number of statutory agencies. It identified a number of perceived gaps in provision:

- lack of coordination/integration of provision;
- lack of affordable childcare options;
- lack of recreational activities for young people;
- lack of activities for children under the age of 10;
- no service provision outside of traditional hours (for example, 9am–5pm);
- few educational programmes for low achievers/early school leavers;
- little assistance with transition from primary to secondary to tertiary level education;
- little support for families and young parents;
- no after-school/drop-in centre for children;
- no outreach work;
- no respite care for parents;
- no care for foreign national young people, especially unaccompanied minors.

The situational analysis also identified a number of difficulties affecting services. These included:

- funding (despite €8 million already supplied for voluntary bodies, plus an unknown sum for the statutory sector);
- lack of staff;
- lack of facilities/premises;
- no coordinated approach;
- aggressive behaviour by children and young people.

This analysis led to a set of strategic goals for the period 2006–09 in order to address the identified issues, and in 2010 the YPAR protocol was launched by the Minister for Children. The protocol is a key step in interagency collaboration, permitting any agency to seek the assistance of any other agency to support a child, young person or a family by calling a case meeting.

An individual care plan is then agreed and implemented by the various actors involved, ensuring that information is shared and action is coordinated between agencies. The protocol creates formal links between the school, family and community services in order to address risks in a systematic and effective way.

With this protocol in place, a new strategic plan was developed to continue with the work until 2014. The goals of this plan are:

- to implement the YPAR protocol so as to facilitate the integration of services that was developed during the 2006–09 period;
- to facilitate and develop young people's participation in YPAR and the transnational element of YEPP in order to give youth an opportunity to impact on decision makers;
- to ensure that the work of YPAR is used to inform service delivery organisations and to shape policy development for young people at risk;
- to ensure that YPAR operates effectively and efficiently.

In order to get this far, YPAR has implemented two YEPP cycles of change and these have been evaluated annually. This process has been supported by other components of the YEPP method, such as the establishment of a local steering group, the appointment of a part-time coordinator, periodic support from evaluation consultants, the development of strategic plans, yearly reviews and the influence of the European dimension on the discussions, as well as the direct impact of the transnational work on young people.

Nevertheless, not everything is a garden of roses. There was lack of attendance at the steering group on the part of some statutory agencies; there was a fear of change, especially with regard to the interagency approach (the YPAR protocol); some goals were not adequately defined; some working groups did not function; a part-time coordinator and associated consultants provided insufficient staff time; and some young people were not committed.

These issues have been readdressed in the current strategic plan of the second cycle 2010–14, with the following major outcomes, which are grouped under four main goals.

Goal 1 – Implementing the protocol

- The YPAR protocol for coordinating services was launched by the Minister for Children, in front of 180 people and 70+ groups.
- The protocol group meets regularly, with agreed work plans and role.
- The use of the protocol expanded significantly in 2020–11, involving the cases of 80+ young people and families and 60+ organisations.
- Over 40 statutory and community organisations have participated in training; there have been several meetings and networking on the use of the protocol, leading to a new interagency way of working with young people.
- A child protection workshop was held for 120 people, with Health Service Executive/interagency presentations.
- A pilot 'Strengthening Families' programme was implemented.
- A protocol coordinator is engaged in on-going support, monitoring, tracking, and review of the use of the protocol in partnership with the protocol working group.

Goal 2: Youth participation

YPAR supported young people to attend the YEPP advocacy training and other transnational events. In addition, six young people attended the Youth Bank training, which led to the establishment of the North East Inner City Youth Bank by a committee of eight young people. Several small grants have been awarded for:

- a youth garden;
- a health and beauty programme in Dublin dockyards;
- a programme for youth leadership in the community;
- a health and fitness programme;
- running development awareness sessions in schools and clubs, following a visit to Zambia.

In addition, drama workshops have led to the creation of a youth forum for the community and the foreign nationals' workshop meets regularly. It organised a programme for 150 foreign national young people in the area.

The foreign nationals have also organised a regular international youth club, they have produced a drugs awareness leaflet in seven languages and have met with the police about combating racist bullying.

The working group for 5- to 12-year-olds has also organised events with interagency support for over 300 young people, it has piloted sessions on the 'Voice of the Child' in two schools and has discussed the safety of play areas and parks with the police. It has also started planning for summer projects, and this has included discussions about a youth cafe.

Goal 3: Advocacy

YPAR has had a large number of meetings with a wide range of agencies about implementing and strengthening the protocol, including with the Office of the Minister for Children and Youth Affairs, the Office for the Minister for Integration and other statutory bodies, as well as with the YEPP Programme Team.

Goal 4: Organisational effectiveness

Following the review of the first cycle, a full-time coordinator was appointed, in addition to the part-time coordinator for the protocol implementation. However, due to the recent cut-backs caused by the financial crisis starting in 2008, the coordinator's position was reduced to a part-time position. The YPAR steering group meets regularly, with tracked attendance; the management sub-committee meets monthly to progress the work of the steering committee and oversee the work of the coordinators; the finance sub-committee meets monthly. YPAR also continues to engage with YEPP and fulfil its requirements as a YEPP Local Programme Site, including participation in evaluation training, with the result that an evaluation facilitator was appointed and an evaluation framework was put in place. Regrettably, this post was discontinued in 2011, following the economic crash.

Conclusion

In conclusion, it is clear that YPAR in collaboration with YEPP and the use of the YEPP approach and methodology have advanced significantly over the past few years, and YPAR's profile with a broad range of stakeholders has been considerably enhanced. YPAR has been especially effective in developing and implementing the interagency working protocol and has used it with a large number of young people, offering more effective services and developing a fuller understanding of interagency working.

A large number of young people, including foreign nationals, have been involved in a wide range of events, including YEPP's transnational activities, the Youth Bank, leisure activities and health and anti-drug initiatives.

YPAR's advocacy programme has been enhanced through the appointment of new staff and it has also influenced communities in the wider Dublin area, especially with regard to interagency working practices.

The European dimension introduced by YEPP has been influential and has allowed YPAR to benchmark its work internationally.

Kristinestad[2]

Kristinestad is situated in the southern part of the Ostrobothnian region in the West Coast Province of Finland. Although, historically, Swedish was the official language, this has been steadily replaced by Finnish over the past few years. Now, the population is bilingual, with slightly more people speaking Swedish than Finnish as a first language. Like many rural areas, it suffers, for example, from the emigration of young people, limited educational opportunities, unemployment, drug and alcohol abuse and cuts in youth services.

Before the start of YEPP work in Kristinestad in 2001, the municipal council had already instigated a project to encourage youth participation in decision making via a Youth Council, and, since that time, many of the YEPP initiatives, such as the Little Parliament and the Youth Parliament, have developed into permanent activities of the Municipal Youth Office. Although the Local Support Group is still supported by some of the original organisations, there have also been many changes, with new organisations coming on board, alongside changes in personnel. However, at times it has proved difficult to continue following the YEPP approach, with a not uncommon tension between practical implementation and bureaucracy. Furthermore, the time available to both the local coordinator and the evaluation facilitator has diminished, meaning that involvement with the Local Support Group has been weakened, and this, in its turn, reduces the scope of YEPP activities.

Despite these developments, the Local Support Group recognises the importance of all parts of YEPP's cycle-of-change approach, namely implementation, monitoring and evaluation, and it has carried out a new situational analysis and developed a new operational plan. These key elements of YEPP have been facilitated by the data collected over the years and held in a log book, and by engagement in other YEPP activities during the YEPP community conferences and on-going interactions with the programme team.

Many of the activities started during the first cycles of YEPP, between 2001 and 2005, have expanded. An outcome of the EmpowerMediaNetwork has been the Youth Channel, which is a TV station where young people make programmes about and for young people. It broadcasts regularly on the local TV station, both for the community and for the region. The Youth Channel remains an active member of the EmpowerMediaNetwork and it also runs local media workshops.

The Local Programme Site also continued its connections with the Little Parliament and initiated the Youth Parliament for young people aged 13–16. This parliament has a greater emphasis than the Little Parliament on how to initiate projects without funding, and the ideas collected are passed on to the Youth Council and the Municipal Youth Office, which redirect them to relevant boards. The Municipal Youth Office has also initiated pupils' council training, so as to teach young people how to debate and vote, take initiatives and speak out about their own feelings, alongside other techniques related to formal meetings.

In the new operational plan there is a focus on intercultural meeting places, the summer job project and the Youth Council. These activities are intended to increase the contact between asylum seekers and the long-term inhabitants of Kristinestad, to help young people to find work during the summer by offering them a summer-job cheque (value €160) and to increase the Youth Council's participation and decision-making powers in the community.

Goal 1: Youth and community empowerment

Since the outset of YEPP, youth and community empowerment had been the most important goal for Kristinestad because of its rural situation and the associated challenges already described. More recently, the Youth Council has become a consulting body of the municipal board and has played a significant role in discussions on areas such as trade and industry, technical planning, health and social care, education and more.

> After the Municipality's election in 2008 the composition of the Municipal Council changed in a positive way. From a total of 27 seats, six young people under the age of 31 were elected to the Municipal Council. One Youth Council member ... 22 years old, was elected both into the Municipal Council (2009–2012) and the Municipal Board (2009–2010). This is seen as a positive outcome of

the long-term youth work within the YEPP framework.
(Bårdsnes-Malinen, 2011, p 13)

There is also a reported stronger sense of community and self-esteem
among the citizens, with pride at the work accomplished. Because
children and young people are now offered more opportunities to take
part in different activities and to be heard and taken seriously, they
contribute and engage more confidently and take more responsibility
for their lives and the environment. Of course, challenges remain, one
of which is to include more Finnish speakers in the work. Reflecting
back on the difficulties of maintaining the work of the Local Support
Group, there is still a need to find a working methodology for this
group so as to keep it alive.

Goal 2: Partnership

AlthoughYEPP began via a partnership of the public and independent
sectors, the situation now is very different. The members of the Local
Support Group are mainly people who work on the ground with youth.
This has threatened the sustainability of the Local Support Group, and
reinvigoration of the group with representatives from other sectors
will be necessary in order to maintain a dynamic. Maintaining the
connection withYEPP and participating regularly in the transnational
YEPP events over the 10 years has helped to keep the exchange
programme with otherYEPP sites alive. This led also to Kristinestad's
own transnational initiatives, for instance, an international workshop
that was held in Kristinestad, and further collaboration with Dublin
through a workshop 'Finland on the Liffey'.[3] There is also collaboration
with a municipality called Porsgrunn in Norway, around TV. More
recently, Kristinestad has become twinned with the village of Novello,
which is part of theYEPP local site of Langhe in Italy. This arrangement
was mediated by the local coordinators in Langhe and Kristinestad.
 Kristinestad has also joined the 'slow city' movement 'Cittaslow'. The
goals of Cittaslow are to improve the quality of life in towns while
resisting 'the fast lane, homogenised world so often seen in other cities
throughout the world' (Bårdsnes-Malinen, 2011, p 15).

Goal 3: Advocacy

Advocacy has been a major part of theYEPP work in Kristinestad since
the outset, and it is clear that this has been successful, since youth now

have significant input into decision making. This is, without doubt, a major impact of YEPP in this community.

It is worth restating the arguments made by the Local Support Group to the municipal council in 2002, to accept the values of the Local Support Group regarding young people so that they can become an integral element of its policy development. These were:

- children and youth are competent individuals;
- all children, not only the resourceful, are entitled to be recognised;
- every child should experience success in everyday life.

The Local Support Group also requested the municipal government and council of Kristinestad to include an emphasis on the following goal in its budget and economic plan for the year 2003:

- To allow the Youth Council to participate in the strategic decision making in the municipality and to take notice of three priority measures:
    - all departments involve the Youth Council in their planning;
    - seek possibilities to give youth more opportunities to impact on the environment; and
    - promote the competence of children and youth to run their own activities and to contribute to change.

That same month, the municipal council agreed to this proposal and the Youth Council is now one of its consultative bodies.

Conclusions

In Kristinestad there has always been a positive policy towards involving youth, and this has certainly been very helpful in promoting YEPP there and has led to a mutually beneficial partnership. There have also been very committed people who have often worked against the odds to make YEPP happen – and without a great deal of financial support. The very positive attitude of the municipality towards involving young people made it easy for it to accept the Local Support Group's proposals to involve youth more fully in policy making, and this decision and its willingness to fund activities through the Youth Office has led to many positive developments for both the community and the young people living there. In this Local Programme Site, YEPP quickly had a major impact on the public services. In this it was supported for a short time by the independent sector, which allowed the Local Support Group to flourish and catalyse new initiatives.

Tuzla-Simin Han[4]

Simin Han is a district in the city of Tuzla in Bosnia and Herzegovina, in south-eastern Europe. Here YEPP first began its work in Tuzla nine years ago, in a community traumatised by war and with many displaced people. Simin Han was receiving considerable but uncoordinated support from many aid sources and there was a perceived need for a more holistic approach.

The YEPP Local Programme Site in Tuzla quickly formed a Local Support Group, which produced an operational plan to focus on promoting youth and community empowerment by:

* helping to reconstruct the damaged/non-existent infrastructure;
* promoting economic, social and cultural development;
* supporting education and training;
* strengthening employability, self-initiative and entrepreneurship;
* supporting social cohesion; and
* promoting active citizenship and community action.

By 2003, Tuzla-Simin Han had established a meeting place called the 'Agora', as well as the Community Foundation Simin Han. The Community Foundation not only became a guarantor for future sustainability of the YEPP approach and methodology, but has become a key player in civil society in Tuzla. When it started working it was based in the Agora centre, and by 2006 had taken over the implementation of YEPP, but still with external funding support.

In 2008 another Tuzla community, Gornja Tuzla, joined YEPP and began to benefit from the activities initiated by the community foundation. With its growing sphere of influence, which also included three other communities in Tuzla – Husino, Solina and Tušanj – the Community Foundation Simin Han became the Community Foundation Tuzla and moved out of the Agora to new offices in the city of Tuzla, where it would be better positioned to influence public policies more effectively. This move did not have any negative influence on the position of the Agora centre as was originally feared. The Agora centre was able to appoint a coordinator and a team of young employees, which strengthened the position of the centre. When the Simin Han primary school increasingly reduced its change-creating role, an independent organisation, Association Agora – Centre for

Community Education and Life-long Learning Tuzla, was established in cooperation with representatives of Simin Han Women's Association and the Local Administration Office.

Even with all of these developments, the Local Support Group still meets regularly in Simin Han and its members are still mostly from the civil society sector, including civil society organisations, public institutions (primarily elementary schools, health centres and community centres), professional organisations such as child education centres, women's organisations, the local community administration and other stakeholders. But, most importantly, they continue to meet regularly, plan, organise and participate in all structured activities in the community (regular Local Support Group meetings, topic-related meetings, locally organised actions, workshops and so on). In 2010, representatives from the business sector became members of the Local Support Group, marking an important new development.

The structure of the Local Support Group in Gornja Tuzla is similar to that of the Simin Han Local Support Group. It meets regularly and it has been able to use the previously unused public cultural centre to expand its activities to the benefit of the local community.

Process

Situation analyses were carried out in both Simin Han and Gornja Tuzla and cycles of change were initiated. These key features of YEPP also occurred in the other three communes that were being supported by the Tuzla Community Foundation. They also set up Local Support Groups with similar representation to those in Simin Han and Gornja Tuzla.

Despite all of these very positive developments, evaluation of the work initiated via the cycles of change was a challenge, especially with regard to the positive and negative outcomes. It would seem that these difficulties made the evaluation post expendable,, and eventually the evaluation facilitator was unable to continue because of lack of funds thus preventing participatory monitoring and evaluation from becoming a central part of the planning of activities established in the two communities.

Community empowerment

The Local Support Groups meet regularly in both YEPP communities, since they find that this is the best way of creating an atmosphere of open communication and effectiveness. Typical activities with the communities include:

- the organisation of seminars and training for civil society groups in Local Programme Sites and other communities; and
- enabling participants to acquire knowledge through practical work, for example, by supporting participants to organise and implement community actions such as improving the ecological status of the community.

In 2010, the number of active citizens participating in the various projects reached a total of 188 in five communities, and all local stakeholders were included. Women and men are equally represented and around 30% of participants are youth under the age of 26.

Seminars and activity planning were conducted in February 2010 in all five communities. Seminars on topics such as civil society, active citizenship and community organising in practice were implemented throughout the year. Local Support Group members regularly exchanged information and cooperated in the implementation of activities and the Tuzla Community Foundation also organized training on specific topics in which local groups were interested, in order to build the capacities of active citizens. During the year, additional training was organised by individual volunteers and associations, including:

- A seminar on the 'Correct Disposal of Plastic Waste, Healthy Family, Healthy Community' was organised prior to the Spring Fair in Simin Han, in order to raise awareness of environmental issues caused by uncontrolled waste disposal. The seminar was conducted by a volunteer, an environmental engineer.
- 'Why Is It Important for Women to Vote?' was organised by the Vesta Association for women members of the association and other women in Simin Han. The goal was to strengthen the role of women in society and motivate more women to vote.
- In October, training in fundraising for the Parents–Teachers Council was organised in Simin Han. The community had a safety problem, as groups of youngsters from Tuzla gather in the school yard during weekends and at night and vandalise the area. The biggest problem is that they leave garbage behind them, including needles and syringes. Therefore the group decided to start fundraising to purchase surveillance cameras for the school. In the training, fundraising methods were introduced to a group of 14 parents and teachers

and a six-month fundraising plan was created. By the end of 2010, the group had raised 20% of the funds they needed for the cameras.

The final event related to community organising activities took place in December 2010. It was a community conference at which all Local Support Groups met and discussed 'Best Practices, Potential Risks and Suggestions for the Future'. The conference took place in Simin Han and there were 51 participants and a further 15 volunteers from Simin Han. The significance of the event was considerable, since joint planning was carried out at the city level for the first time. There were also guests from other communities, who urged that the process be disseminated to other communities in need.

The final conclusions were that it was very beneficial to have regular meetings and planning at the level of the community and that cooperation between local government (local community councils) and civil sector organisations is vital for this process. The recommendations were to disseminate community organising training to all 40 local community councils and stakeholders, in order to build local community development groups across the city. In the aftermath, a meeting with the municipality was organised and the deputy mayor in charge of local community councils strongly supported this approach and offered to help in the implementation process .

The local community groups of Gornja Tuzla and Simin Han sent representatives to the fourth YEPP Community Conference and Youth Meeting in Genoa in 2010, titled 'Be the Change', including four young representatives from both project sites, a president of the municipal council and a Youth Bank representative. The event was attended by over 150 people from eight European countries. They exchanged information and experience and discussed issues such as 'the role of youth in society and the challenges they face in Europe today'. The fact that a person from the Tuzla municipal council participated in the conference contributed to the visibility of YEPP and the Tuzla Community Foundation, and their presence may well have a positive impact on cooperation with the municipal administration in the future.

Agora community centre

The Agora has been a key element in the development of YEPP in Simin Han from the outset, and its importance has grown over the years. The Agora is always available for the citizens of Simin Han, to exchange information and strengthen communication and partnerships inside the community. It provides opportunities for non-formal education, revitalising the community socially and promoting volunteerism.

The community education programme 2010 was highly successful and marked an increase in the number of informal courses offered by the centre (39 courses with over 500 participants). Regular annual activities, the spring fair and open days were also successfully carried out, with 24 organisations and citizens' groups presenting their work at the fair, and five Agora open days, when all groups active in the centre to prepared activities, workshops and seminars for children, youth, women and the elderly. Approximately 450 stakeholders were present, with 900 participants.

The transformation of the Agora community centre into an independent association 'Agora' in 2011:

> serves as the best example of community empowerment in Simin Han. It is the result of the empowerment of the community residents who came to feel positively enough about themselves, their community, their capacities to feel comfortable owning a hub of positive change that Agora has always been. Interestingly, Agora will now be placed into the hands of those whose empowerment it enabled, and it can be said that the community and youth empowerment process has come full circle in this case. (Tuzla Community Foundation Programme Staff Members, 2011, p 10)

The influence of the Agora community centre has extended well beyond Simin Han to the other communities involved. It is expected that, in time, the citizens in these other communities will realise the import role that community centres can play in generating positive outcomes.

While such facilities may seem commonplace to those living in western democracies, it is important to appreciate that in a country like Bosnia and Herzegovina, where in the recent past everything was organised by a centralised government and people came to accept that everything is somebody else's responsibility, citizen involvement through centres such as the Agora represents a major development.

Youth empowerment

The Youth Bank was initiated by the Tuzla Community Foundation early in the development of YEPP Simin Han and now includes the following regular activities:

- organisation of Youth Bank training for new members so that they can become grant makers – this covers project evaluation and decision making;
- fortnightly meetings of the Youth Bank board (whose members change every year);
- mentoring the process of grant making, monitoring and evaluation.

In total, 56 small groups and organisations applied for funds during the year and the Youth Bank board members met with them all and made 18 awards totalling €4,800.

In 2009, the Youth Bank board began supporting the Tuzla Reference Group, a network of non-governmental organisations, through a project to renovate municipal office space leased to the Reference Group. This important network had almost ceased to exist, and the support was necessary. Under the leadership of the Tuzla Community Foundation, the Tuzla Reference Group committed to developing a youth strategy and plan, the first one to be adopted by the Tuzla municipality, which was a major step towards influencing youth policies in Tuzla.

> This project represented an excellent example of how Youth Bank not only supports youth initiatives but can spread its 'scope of work' onto solving or, more exactly, 'filling in' for the support that should have come from the public sector in Tuzla. (Tuzla Community Foundation Programme Staff Members, 2011, p 10)

Youth Councils were established in both YEPP programme sites, Simin Han and Gorjna Tuzla, and began to implement activities either in collaboration with other Local Support Group members or *ab initio*, all of which had been included in the agreed operational plan. Later, Youth Councils also formed in other local communities supported by the Tuzla Community Foundation.

One of the priorities of the YEPP-related work in Tuzla has been leadership workshops in which around 110 children aged 9–14 participated, animated by 22 young leaders aged 15–22.

It is estimated that these various innovations and activities of the Community Foundation Tuzla reached some 2,000 young people in Simin Han, Gorjna Tuzla and the other three communities involved. In all five of the communities, the local community councils (which have youth representation from Simin Han and Gorjna) now take account of the opinions and recommendations of the youth councils. These young people will soon be able to serve on the City Youth Council that will be established following a new youth policy law passed in 2009.

Advocacy

Through the Agora, local citizens in Simin Han had an opportunity to participate in an analysis of changes to a municipal statute, to be forwarded to the Statutory Commission. The Local Support Group proposed that the statute be changed so that candidates for election to the local council need no longer be members of political parties and, furthermore, that young people themselves should also have the opportunity to be elected. It is almost certainly not coincidental that Simin Han was the only community in Tuzla to have such a discussion. As a result, representatives were invited to meet with the Statutory Commission and present their views, which in turn led to a revised proposal being presented to the city council for adoption.

A different example of effective lobbying applies to the elementary school in Solina. This school needed new boilers for winter heating, but there were insufficient funds. Following an appeal by the head teacher to the Local Support Group, pressure was put on the administration to find a solution and this eventually led to the boilers' being replaced. This successful outcome came about because of regular cooperation and networking within the community, which was initiated by YEPP.

Another relevant example is the result of the work of the Tuzla Reference Group, in which the Tuzla Community Foundation played a significant role. The Tuzla Community Foundation led the Working Group for Youth Issues and initiated the process of developing a youth strategy for the Tuzla municipality. The draft of the Youth Strategy 2011–2013 was submitted to the Municipal Department for Social Affairs in March 2010. Employment and youth entrepreneurship, youth education, youth health and social care, youth participation and free time were identified as priorities:

> Unfortunately, due to the political crisis and the elections in October 2010, the Youth Strategy for Tuzla Municipality has not as yet been discussed or approved. Recent adoption

of the Youth Law for Federation of Bosnia and Herzegovina helped us to further push Tuzla Municipal Government to get back to the draft document. In 2011, TCF [Tuzla Community Foundation] was invited by Municipal government to work together on the revision of the draft which was finally finished in October 2011. The revised document will be submitted to Tuzla Municipal Council in late 2011. (Tuzla Community Foundation Programme Staff Members, 2011, p 15)

Key messages[5]

- Bottom-up mobilisation of young people and citizens is particularly effective for empowering communities in post-conflict environments.
- Young people can participate actively in creating sustainable change only if opportunities for civic and community engagement are open to them and regular training is provided.
- Community initiatives launched and managed by local residents ensure ownership, responsibility and the empowerment of community actors.
- Youth empowerment and community development are long-term processes that regularly require new inputs, good supporting structures and determination to bring about change.

Antwerp North[6]

Antwerp North is a multi-ethnic neighbourhood in the city of Antwerp, Belgium with many social problems. The condition of its housing stock is well below average and there are high levels of poverty, and tensions between the older Belgian residents and new immigrants. The levels of street crime and unemployment are high, with some 75% of North African young people being out of work. There are few indoor meeting places, meaning that the streets are used for recreation, much to the annoyance of older residents.

Community empowerment

Antwerp North experienced some difficulty in developing as a YEPP Local Programme Site during YEPP I. However, the decision to invite RISO, and its on-going link with *Burtschatten* ('neighbourhood treasures'), was a key decision, and in YEPP II the YEPP programme was completely merged with *Burtschatten*. The 'Can-Do' approach

(Scarman Trust, 2007) helped to mobilise local citizens to engage in shaping their neighbourhood. This organisation has grown substantially over the years and now has a fund that follows the principles of a community foundation. This fund is managed by community residents and regularly evaluates the way in which it functions. It is now seeking financial support from the private sector and the project is being established in other parts of the city. The Evens Foundation, which supports the work in this Local Programme Site, has exported the model to a suburb of Paris.

Youth empowerment

Currently, however, the Burtschatten Campaign Fund, which is equivalent to the Local Support Group, does not include many young people. In view of this, it has an active policy to attract them, using three main initiatives. First, it engages with other organisations working in the youth sector, in an effort to link its focus on local residents and their interests to those of young people, and it has had some success to this end. Second, it approaches young people on the street, but with very limited success; and third, it cooperates with schools. This last approach has had limited success but there is currently a project involving several schools that are setting up a youth parliament so that youth will have a voice in the local elections in 2012.

Partnerships

Over time it has proved difficult to maintain the impetus of the *Burtschatten* approach, which means that there is always a need to find new projects and to maintain connections between its members. Evaluation has proved useful in this regard, since it provides more objective evidence on how the project functions. For example, discussions about obtaining private sector funds led to a realisation that many businesses are involved in an ad hoc way and that there was a need to try to engage more local businesses and bigger enterprises to become involved in a more structured way.

Advocacy

Local politicians and senior officials in the city of Antwerp are invited to all local activities and a dialogue between the mayor and young people has begun. A local 'project fair' was organised that proved very successful in drawing the attention of the public sector to the *Burtschatten* philosophy.

The main contribution of YEPP in Antwerp North has been the transnational element, which proved to be a very important incentive for young people, encouraging them to engage in the work. This element of YEPP also opened the way to introducing a European dimension into local initiatives, which introduced new people to the local process and enabled young people to be better heard by the local administration. YEPP has helped Antwerp to learn from others and this has provided considerable impetus to continue.

Conclusion

It is clear that Antwerp had difficulty from the outset in becoming a fully fledged YEPP Local Programme Site, and it remains an interested observer willing to 'cherry pick' ideas developed in other YEPP sites. There have been developments in the community, such as a new park that includes areas for young people, a new city library with a cafe, an auditorium and a meeting place. A swimming pool has recently opened with a brasserie, hamam and other steam baths. There are also many other events. Unfortunately it is impossible to say whether YEPP had any impact on these developments. They might well have happened anyway. But YEPP clearly had an influence on the developments in Antwerp North and some of its ideas and working methods have been absorbed, to the benefit of local people.

Turin-Mirafiori[7]

Turin-Mirafiori is a suburb of the city of Turin, recently industrialised as a result of the expansion of FIAT motor cars. There has been no growth in the population since the 1980s and there are high levels of unemployment, with associated problems of substance abuse, street gangs and so on. More recently, however, issues related to social risk and deviancy have changed and decreased.

As reported in Chapter Three, Mirafiori was a well-implemented YEPP site and many of the organisations that formed the Local Support Group are still involved. In addition, and as reported there, at the end of YEPP I the beginnings of a self-funding programme were visible, so that by 2006–07 the supporting foundation provided only 50% of the necessary funds for YEPP II. The remainder came from a variety of sources, including the public sector.

Perhaps as a result of the success of YEPP I, the transition to YEPP II was fairly smooth and, based on the evaluation results, the Local Support Group decided to continue with the three main areas of work – community media, the economic incubator and self-organisation. The main goals were:

- the active involvement of young people at all levels of the development of and involvement in projects;
- the improvement of Mirafiori's image, in order to attract people from outside;
- opening up further economic and employment opportunities;
- the growth of cultural activities for all residents.

At the commencement of YEPP II, the main decision made by the Local Support Group was to create a Mirafiori community foundation, in order to support new projects by developing YEPP's principles more completely and becoming a central player in the social, economic and educational development of the local community, with special concern for youth policies.

Following the agreement in principle to establish the foundation, there were lengthy discussions about its constitution, in the context of Italian law, between the Compagnia di San Paolo and the city of Turin. The idea of creating a general assembly, comprising a large number of representatives of the local community, with consulting and decision-making powers proved impossible. Finally it was agreed to follow the traditional route of establishing a political board and an executive board, with the Local Support Group becoming a second-level organisation to be known as 'Miravolante'. The Compagnia di San Paolo would continue to fund the foundation along with the city, whose support would replace that of the local development agency.

It is immediately clear that this community foundation has a formality far greater than that of the Local Support Group. Members of the governing board are Miravolante, the Compagnia di San Paolo, the city of Turin, Mirafiori District, Turin University, the Catholic Church and the Chamber of Commerce. The chairman was a member of the council of the Compagnia di San Paolo. The YEPP local coordinator became the director, but only for a short period, since he preferred to work in the field rather than in management.

The mission of the foundation is to promote the improvement of the environment and of social life in Mirafiori by fundraising and by supporting actions and projects proposed and run by local people.

Within this structure there are four 'institutional projects' managed directly by the foundation and a number of local projects funded by it.
   The institutional projects are:

- Park House: a building built by the city and given to the community foundation to run. One part of the building is a meeting and working space open to local organisations and residents and the other part is a café-restaurant run by an organisation selected via a competitive bidding procedure.
- Homework House: to support students in their first two years of high school with their studies, as well as social and sporting activities during the summer vacation.
- Social Office: support to residents to facilitate access to services.
- Youth Bank: to support youth-led projects via a competitive process.

The foundation also supported a number of projects of local organisations:

- radio and theatre activities at the youth centre;
- summer leisure-time initiatives for young people aged 14 to 18;
- participation in planning a regenerated area around the local river for kitchen gardens and green spaces;
- social activities in the street;
- a family centre providing opportunities to meet and for families with small children to socialise and to receive counselling when necessary;
- a project aimed at preventing drug and alcohol abuse.

It is clear that the former Local Support Group, now Miravolante, saw the foundation as a natural progression of YEPP, providing greater stability and embedding the working style it had developed over the previous years. Its formation took up a great deal of time and energy, with the result that important aspects of YEPP II, such as the evaluation of the third action cycle, did not take place. Despite the local researcher's being put in charge of the evaluation of the foundation, with support for its importance being given by the Local Support Group, and evaluation proposals' being made, these were neither agreed on nor implemented.

Youth empowerment

The extent of youth engagement has been an important indicator of the success of YEPP in Mirafiori, with mixed results. Young people with more education and social skills participated more fully. Those less skilled participated less. For example, 10 street children participated in the Mirafuori TV project but, although this outcome is positive, their level of participation was limited to being involved regularly in the project but not in its planning. This may be contrasted with the involvement of two university students who took responsibility for the projects and also acted as coaches to the street children. However, they did not participate in the overall planning of Mirafuori TV.

The YEPP principles also influenced the working style of the youth centre, where joint planning between those responsible for the centre and the YEPP Local Support Group has always occurred. One outcome has been the Youth Bank, which has empowered those young people involved, leading to their becoming very autonomous. The criteria for the selection of projects by the Youth Bank embody YEPP's principles of active involvement of young people, partnership between organisations, active involvement of the project's beneficiaries, the presence of transnational partners and rigorous evaluation.

Community empowerment

Through the use of cycles of change and evaluation, YEPP provided a mechanism for the Local Support Group to operate within, and this was often stated during evaluation meetings. It empowered the group through capacity building, giving the members new skills and increased confidence. However, on the downside, not enough members of the local population were involved in the projects, but this is an issue that the community foundation will be able to address more fully.

Partnership

In general, the results here were very positive. There was networking between independent organisations and steps were taken to build partnerships between non-profit organisations and the public sector. YEPP saw an increase in cooperation between the Local Support Group and the district administration at both high and low levels – the district president and local politicians, and with the municipality. These relations with the public sector were a precondition for inclusion in the community foundation.

Advocacy

The local district and its president have always been active supporters of YEPP I and II, due to its perceived value for the community and young people because of the promotion of YEPP by the local coordinator and the Local Support Group. As a result, the goals and principles of YEPP have become a part of public thinking and action at city and local levels. YEPP has helped to overcome earlier fragmented policies and practices through its working methods and, of course, the strong and continuing support of the Compagnia di San Paolo.

Conclusions

YEPP has had a very substantial impact on Turin-Mirafiori, culminating in the creation of the community foundation based on partnership. This is a particular achievement in the Italian context, where there have always been tensions between more powerful and weaker partners over decision making. As we have seen in the development of the Mirafiori community foundation, the strong members showed no interest in adopting the evaluation principles that were so strongly supported by the weaker member, that is, the Local Support Group. The question that now remains is how strongly the community foundation will be anchored in the community of Mirafiori. We shall have to wait to see what the future holds.

Expanding YEPP within countries

Italy

The close involvement of the Compagnia di San Paolo with the development of YEPP in Turin led it to decide to support the expansion of YEPP in north-western Italy in two regions, Piedmont and Liguria, in partnership with the various municipalities. These Local Programme Sites are far from being homogeneous and cover communities where there have been major changes in the economy, as in Turin-Mirafiori with the fall and rebirth of the FIAT motor company and in Genoa-Cornigliano with the closure of the steel industry. These may be contrasted with the rural vineyards of Langhe, the agriculture and tourism of Albenga, the summer holiday resort of Loano and the fishing port of La Spezia. Currently YEPP is being implemented in this part of Italy in these six Local Programme Sites and one affiliate site – The Gate in Turin Porta Palazzo.

Although there are major differences between these communities in terms of their economic structures, there are many similarities in their social problems. Many of them have multi-ethnic populations and/or immigrant workers, which creates tensions, and they all need to create additional constructive employment and leisure opportunities for young people, with drug and alcohol abuse being a significant concern.

Learning from YEPP I, Compagnia di San Paolo approached this regional expansion through discussions with the municipalities and locally operating (community) foundations, not just to encourage them to take part in YEPP and approach sustainability but also to share the costs. This led to the posts of coordinator and evaluation facilitator being met by each municipality concerned, while the activity and transnational costs were provided by Compagnia di San Paolo and a few smaller foundations. In addition, Compagnia di San Paolo funded the work of a YEPP-experienced support team for all Italian YEPP sites that had been involved already in YEPP I, as local coordinators and local researchers.

Furthermore, the inherent flexibility of the YEPP approach allowed a number of different implementation structures to emerge. For instance, in Genoa-Cornigliano the city of Genoa and the local municipality are involved; in Langhe it comprises a partnership of eight villages; in La Spezia two districts are taking part; while the other Local Programme Sites include only a single municipal administration.

Despite these substantial variations in community structure, YEPP has been implemented in a very similar way. In the terminology of the assessment presented in Chapter Three, all are well-implemented sites. That is, local coordinators and evaluation facilitators have been appointed and Local Support Groups including young people have been created. In addition, situation analyses have been carried out, action plans formulated and cycles of change initiated and evaluated. The Local Support Groups also vary considerably in their membership. In Loano the group consists entirely of young people, while in Genoa-Cornigliano social cooperatives that were born during the area's industrial past and religious organisations are working together.

With these variations in local structure, history and culture the detailed outcomes of YEPP in these Local Programme Sites all vary. In Langhe, for example, the eight village administrations joined forces to create additional spaces for youth activities and have begun to develop a shuttle service between the villages, since there is no local transport and driving while under the influence of alcohol is a problem. They have worked on sporting events, the EmpowerMediaNetwork and on developing a Youth Bank. These initiatives are all intended to:

> involve a greater number of young people in local community life, to empower them to plan and manage activities, to develop their communication and advocacy

skills, and to raise awareness of youth issues among local decision-makers. (10 Years of YEPP Policy Folder, 2011 – Langhe[8])

In Genoa–Cornigliano the focus was to establish:

> a 'creativity desk' to attract young people and organise a number of thematic labs on modern forms of artistic expression (music, dance, street art, and so on). A wider project was then launched under the name 'Cornigliano Mon Amour ... nel Tempo' (Cornigliano My Love ... a History) to collect the memories and stories of the area's inhabitants and capture them in a multi-media gallery, which was then displayed in a popular location. This allowed members of the community to share their visions of Cornigliano over the years and create a sense of belonging and social cohesion at a time of significant change. (10 Years of YEPP Policy Folder, 2011 – Genoa–Cornigliano[9])

At the affiliate site in Turin, 'The Gate', even though there has been a history of coordinated youth work, YEPP's model of creating a Local Support Group and developing cycles of change were implemented and, via involvement with the transnational component, there have been a number of significant developments. In addition to cultural events these have led to events for young people in critical places where 'illegal activities often took place' (Brossa, 2010, p 9). The group has also initiated a website and working opportunities for young people in Europe's largest street market, which has taken place every week since 1856.

Some Local Programme Sites have begun to support education. In Albenga immigrants are offered the opportunity to learn Italian so as to help with their integration, and in La Spezia an educational centre has been set up to help children with difficulties and to complement the formal education system.

In Loano, young people in partnership with the municipality and other local partners established the Officina delle Arti (Art Laboratory) in 2008.

> Free courses have been offered to young people aged 12–25 in a number of creative fields: drawing, music, photography, theatre, TV and web community projects ... The objectives of the various activities are to increase youth participation in

Loano, reduce social isolation and raise self-esteem through new forms of expression. (10 Years of YEPP Policy Folder – 2011 Loano[10])

An important ingredient of the well-implemented YEPP approach has been that delegates from all Italian sites participated regularly and actively in YEPP's transnational events. Two of the five YEPP community conferences and youth meetings took place in Italy: 2006 in Turin, 2010 in Genoa.

In 2011 the local coordinators and evaluation facilitators of the YEPP sites in Italy established an independent not-for-profit organisation, YEPP Italy, as a professional support network. One of the first activities of this organisation will be training for young people who have been involved in YEPP for some time to become coaches for the next generation of young people in the local sites. This peer-to-peer approach is seen as a good methodology for further strengthening the empowerment of young people.

Conclusion

The expansion of YEPP in north-western Italy shows how a knowledgeable foundation can support substantial changes simultaneously in many different types of community through the creation of key partnerships with the public sector and other independent organisations.

It also shows how knowledge and experiences can be transferred from local sites that were assessed as well implemented to new sites, in order to achieve a successful implementation of the YEPP approach.

Furthermore, in all of these examples young people have played a key role in creating new structures and activities that can be tailor-made to meet their interests and talents across a wide range of non-formal educational interests. Having many sites working together in these two regions also helps to sustain the efforts in each individual community and to give them a stronger voice vis-à-vis decision makers.

Cooperation across a national frontier

Görlitz/Zgorzelec[11]

Görlitz and Zgorzelec are two towns on either side of the river border between Germany and Poland. Before the end of the Second World War they were a single town within Germany. After the break-up of the Soviet Union the two towns signed a partnership agreement. While there is some common planning in areas such as town planning, environmental protection, culture, sports, education and policing, recent economic difficulties on both sides of the border have led to increased levels of youth unemployment and associated high levels of emigration, especially of graduates and skilled workers.

This situation has led to tensions between the two communities, apathy among the remaining young people and frustrations with 'conservative educational institutions unable to channel their energy into constructive activities for the community.'[12] Cross-border cooperation is also hindered by a decline in youth work, 'Differences in social structures, education models, mentality, nationality, language and culture' (Beltle, 2011, p 4) and the perception that plans are made in Görlitz in Germany and then delivered as *faits accomplis* to the Polish neighbours in Zgorzelec. YEPP was welcomed in the two cities because it was seen as 'neutral player' and has been supported by the Robert Bosch Foundation. Operational support in the two communities is provided through youth organisations in each town.

From the outset, YEPP's approach was seen to challenge the traditional practices in the existing youth organisations in both towns, which generally devised projects and then looked for interest in the communities. A local coordinator was appointed in each town and, for a period of time, one evaluation facilitator for both towns. A situation analysis was carried out by young people and local stakeholders. This identified a lack of cycling lanes, indoor meeting spaces, sports, cultural and entertainment facilities and voluntary service, after-school help, project work beyond school, youth exchange and opportunities for participation to be paramount in Zgorzelec. However, in Görlitz difficulties in finding apprenticeships and work, insufficient leisure and entertainment facilities and a lack of dialogue with local officials were more pervasive. Both groups agreed that there should be more cross-border youth exchange and cooperation. This all led to the creation of a website to promote youth activities in both cities.

There was great enthusiasm in planning for the first cycle of change. However, this waned and the development of the work was left to the local coordinators and the evaluation facilitator and a few core groups, with the result it has proved difficult to establish a formal YEPP Local Support Group. Nevertheless, as confidence and recognition by the public sector in both towns grew, the scene was being set for further developments. At the beginning of the second year more young people joined and now the conditions exist for 'achieving the intended goal of *cross-national self-initiated participation of young people*' (Beltle, 2011, p 8). A youth parliament already existed in Görlitz, and involved youth had already travelled to other EU countries under the auspices of the International Youth Parliament. This inspired the local coordinator and partners in Zgorzelec to initiate their own youth parliament. Through YEPP contacts, the founding of the youth parliament in Zgorzelec was also attended by two students from the Local Programme Site in Slovakia, funded by the EU Erasmus travel grant system for higher education.

YEPP has been very influential in these two towns in developing cross-border collaboration. In the Polish town the public sector institutions have been very supportive and the mayor agreed to create the youth parliament. This contrasted with the situation in Görlitz, where the public sector rather reluctantly agreed to be involved in the work. However, because the local coordinators and the evaluator established a good relationship the process moved forward and now a joint youth parliament is being planned. Furthermore, a successful partnership was developed with the German–Polish Youth Work Organisation and the Foundation for German–Polish Cooperation, which funded part of the situation analysis.

In developing YEPP Görlitz/Zgorzelec, the role of the YEPP Programme Team is viewed in the communities as being especially important. It has been able to coach and train the local actors and has helped to maintain positive attitude and momentum towards achieving the intended goals. In addition, it has helped to get financial support without which the work would not have taken place.

YEPP has been seen as a means to create synergies rather than as a competitor, and the importance of this Local Programme Site to the future development of YEPP was confirmed by the holding of the 5th YEPP Community Conference and Youth Meeting in the two towns in November 2011.

Conclusions

YEPP Görlitz/Zgorzelec is without doubt a challenging Local Programme Site with many structural and attitudinal issues to overcome, and the developments have been modest and mainly linked to the creation of a youth parliament. The extension of this to a German–Polish youth parliament, in collaboration with a Czech partner, and associated activities is an agreed goal to be attained over the next five years.

It is clear that little or no progress would have been made in these two towns using the available youth organisations and methods of working. YEPP's approach, allied to the independent consultancy role that the YEPP Programme Team plays, has been instrumental in creating a constructive start in this Local Programme Site. Furthermore, the confidence in the YEPP programme within the foundation sector has allowed the programme team to leverage funds for this site, something that hitherto would have been unlikely to happen.

Including Roma in Slovakia

Kecerovce-Olšava[13]

This Local Programme Site focuses on the four neighbouring villages of Rankovce, Boliarov, Vtáčkovce and Kererovce in the micro-region of Kecerovce-Olšava in Slovakia. Many Roma families live in these villages, alongside non-Roma families, and the problems experienced by young people have been the focus of discussion in both public and independent sectors. Many programmes have been implemented covering education, artistic activities and local community development. It was YEPP's holistic approach and methodology that attracted the Austrian ERSTE Stiftung to support the establishment of a YEPP Programme Site to explore further the possibilities for the inclusion of the Roma. The local stakeholders in the area wished to capitalise by helping the YEPP Programme Site to structure its activities more effectively. The region has high rates of poverty and unemployment, low levels of education, a low average age in comparison to the rest of Slovakia and poor infrastructure.

Recently the social gap between different groups of youth has been widening. The education results of some have been declining; for others they have been rising, with attendance at upper secondary school and university. However, others drop out at the end of primary school and 'hang out', frequently taking drugs of various sorts.

YEPP began in Kecerovce-Olšava in 2010 following discussions between the YEPP Programme Team and the local Civil Association Centre for Community Development and following a motivating experience at a YEPP community conference. The work began with a situational analysis, which was completed in 2011. And although as of this writing there is no Local Support Group, two local coordinators and two evaluation facilitators (Roma and non-Roma) have been appointed. They have introduced YEPP to the local inhabitants in order to identify the most significant issues that need to be addressed, to propose constructive solutions and to invite further cooperation. Those involved in these discussions included:

active members of the local Roma communities ... youth
workers (community workers and their assistants, social
workers and their assistants, health workers and their
assistants, teaching assistants), representatives of local self-
governments, primary schools and detached workplaces
of secondary schools, representatives of churches and
representatives of NGOs in the micro-region. (Šiňanská,
2011, p 10)

The situational analysis revealed that there were a lack of things for
young people to do and a lack of places that could be used to meet
their needs. For instance, some wanted more emphasis on education
so that the young people could develop their potential and contribute
more fully to their community and society at large. Others wanted
places to meet, with a fitness centre and where they can play music and
put on shows. Yet others would like a multi-purpose sports centre. In
addition, there is a lack of space in the local primary schools, sometimes
necessitating two shifts.

Following the publication of the situational analysis the local
stakeholders met to develop an operational plan. It was agreed to focus
on two main themes:

- 'intensifying leisure-time offers for youngsters'; and
- 'raising motivation for education' (Šiňanská, 2011, p 18).

But, in addition, it was recognised that there was a need to develop
'strong and independent groups of young people who can be
cooperation partners for the local NGOs, but also partners for local
self-government in planning the development of their community'.

In June and July 2011 a project the 'Big Talent Show' was put on with
young people, 'the goal of which was to raise funds for the development
of the youth group, their education as well as for two community
events' (Šiňanská, 2011, p 18).

Youth empowerment

YEPP will build on already existing community programmes in this
region and the training that has already taken place of young people
from all four villages. This has helped the youth to develop skills as
animators and leaders of youth clubs and they have been involved in
planning and evaluating activities, and in communicating with village
leaders and the organisations that work in them.

Community empowerment

Representatives from different sectors have met to discuss the problems of young people, to contribute to the situation analysis, to identify how the problems of young people are perceived and to identify solutions, which led to the creation of an informal platform for cooperation among organisations.

Advocacy

The situational analysis leading to the operational plan is 'one of the first tools for advocacy activities aimed at improving the lives of young people living in this region' (Šiňanská, 2011, p 19).

Conclusion

Although the work in Kecerovce-Olšava has only just begun it has already started to show promising results in communities that are traditionally very difficult to integrate. A key message has already emerged from the work: 'Ideas and content for activities are generated regardless of levels of social exclusion once dedicated time and space are created to develop community initiatives' (10 Years of YEPP Policy Folder, 2011 – Kecerovce-Olšava).

Another sign of good progress was the active participation of a group of Roma young people and the mayor of Kecerovce in the YEPP community conference and youth meeting in Görlitz-Zgorzelec in November 2011.

Interim evaluation 2009

In June 2010, YEPP II presented its overall interim evaluation report (Katsbert and Strocka, 2010), based on the new evaluation approach and drawing on several data sources such as the local interim evaluation reports of the Local Programme Sites, the evaluation of the work of the YEPP Programme Team, evaluations of YEPP transnational activities, site visit reports by members of the YEPP Programme Team and minutes of steering committee meetings.

The report was structured according to the steps of the participatory YEPP monitoring and evaluation design: context, inputs, process, outputs and outcomes that were in line with the YEPP cycle of change. At each step, the local level, the regional/national level and the transnational level of YEPP were evaluated separately. The report closed with a summary of the main findings with regard to the achievement of YEPP's overall goals, lessons learnt and the way forward. The report gave a first structured insight into the progress made during YEPP II.

The achievement of YEPP's overall programme goals was characterised by a number of aspects, including the following (Katsbert and Strocka, 2010, pp 60–61).

Youth and community empowerment

YEPP's overall goal of youth and community empowerment was the main focus of the activities organised by the Local Support Groups in YEPP programme sites. These activities were centred on youth empowerment in social, cultural and educational areas, as well as promoting active citizenship.

In the course of engagement with YEPP, some local stakeholders expanded the focus of their activities to include young people as their new target audience and/or enabled them to participate in the decision-making process as members of the Local Support Groups.

According to the outcome evaluation results, the work of the Local Support Groups contributed to: 'an increase in youth participation in decision making, more opportunities for young people to express their voices and make themselves heard, higher level of young people's self-esteem and the reinforcement of their local identity' (Katsbert and Strocka, 2010, p 60).

Within the YEPP network, supportive tools for youth empowerment were particularly evidenced by the various opportunities for young people to initiate and run their own activities, the establishment of local Youth Banks and the YEPP Transnational Youth Fund, the local and regional advocacy activities of young people – that is, their participation in youth councils and advocacy groups – and the media work within the framework of the EmpowerMediaNetwork, which transformed the voices of young people into images. One special YEPP criterion of empowerment was the involvement of young people in the monitoring and evaluation of their project activities. This gave them ownership of some working results and strengthened their intellectual capacities.

While only a few sites had an explicit focus on community empowerment (for example, Tuzla, Antwerp North), the representation of different citizen groups in the Local Support Groups and their direct engagement in youth- and community-oriented actions contributed to community empowerment. In cases where the Local Support Group was made up of only young people (for example, Loano, Italy) the youth activities helped in reaching and empowering local ethnic and economic minority groups that are part of the local community (for example, migrants in Italy, unemployed youth in Poland). In turn, the community provided a supportive environment for young people's actions, as well as resources and know-how.

Partnership

Beside the partnership of the core group of foundations, the NEF, the INA and OECD/CERI, YEPP's overall goal of partnership proved to be best promoted by the Local Support Groups themselves. The Local Support Group model can be regarded as a 'best practice tool' for a sustainable cross-sectoral partnership in which different stakeholders from the local NGOs, foundations, municipalities and residents are united by common goals, actions, reflections and results. However, the level of involvement of the private sector remained somewhat low, and there remains a need to strengthen public-private partnership. Also, the participation of local authorities in the Local Support Groups' activities varies according to the political culture in the country and their involvement in YEPP from the very beginning. In some Local Programme Sites this remains a challenge.

Apart from cross-sectoral and multi-level partnership, the Local Support Groups also provided the opportunities for inter-generational cooperation, which was appreciated by both young people and adults in most of the Local Programme Sites. The Local Support Group members in Våståboland, Finland, for example, believed that collaboration of young people and adults made a difference because, in the past, things were designed by adults for young people, with little involvement of the latter, and had a lesser outreach effect. Within YEPP, working together was of mutual benefit: young people often needed the support of adults and their guidance while planning and implementing their own projects, whereas the adults could profit from new ideas and the energy of their younger counterparts.

Advocacy

With regard to YEPP's third overall goal of advocacy, the evaluation showed that some of the local administrations had adopted the YEPP approach in designing their youth policies – for example, in Italy and Bosnia and Herzegovina. In Finland the YEPP approach enhanced and strengthened existing youth policies by shifting the focus from doing something *for* the young people to adopting an inter-generational approach to doing it together *with* the young people. Another influence resulted in the promotion of youth initiatives in which young people develop and implement innovations with young people and for young people.

In Italy, the regional governments of Piedmont and Liguria, where most of the YEPP programme sites are located, took great interest in the YEPP approach and established youth participation in decision-making processes on those aspects of youth policies for which they are responsible.

But, by the end of 2009, not all the YEPP sites had formulated policy messages that they wanted to advocate for. Not all of them, in particular the new ones, underwent the whole cycle of change and/or trained the young people in advocacy strategies, following the training of trainers in Gollwitz, in November 2009.

Most advocacy activities were planned to start in 2010, at the local and regional levels. It was anticipated that these would be enhanced by the transnational advocacy strategy, which sought to create synergies between stakeholders of all sectors and promote YEPP's 10-year programme results at the local, regional, national and transnational levels. At the end of the second phase, the presentation of the results of 10 years of YEPP was planned to target, in particular, strategic partners such as politicians, foundations and institutions of the European Union and other key policy makers. Based on the results of the evaluation of YEPP I and II, the partners prepared dissemination and advocacy materials and events in order to further advocate for systemic change in policies on social inclusion.

Comments on the implementation of the new evaluation design

A number of lessons learnt from the evaluation were identified in the reports. The local interim evaluation reports differed in quality. It was recognised that this was a result of the different levels of evaluation experience that the evaluation facilitators had, as well as of the different amounts of time made available, different funding possibilities for the positions of the evaluation facilitators and the commitments of the local teams. This helped in understanding which sites needed additional support with the evaluation, as well as what needed to be done to further strengthen an evaluation culture.

The aim of having an annual report, on the assumption that the local cycles of change would be accomplished in a calendar year, was not achieved. As a result, in some of the programme sites the outcomes had not been assessed by the required time of reporting. This indicates that more flexibility needs to be introduced.

The intended involvement of young people in the monitoring processes turned out to be very challenging for some Local Programme Sites. As a consequence, some sites used monitoring tools other than those proposed in the manual. This indicated that more youth-oriented tools and other ways of increasing young people's motivation to engage in the monitoring and evaluation needed to be developed and incorporated into the manual.

It became obvious that more face-to-face meetings and regular reflections on the evaluation process were needed, in order to strengthen peer learning and support, as well as exchanges of experiences across the programme sites.

Ten years of YEPP, 2001–11

After 10 years of successful work, YEPP as a foundation-led programme came to an end in June 2011. In 2010, the YEPP community agreed on a dissemination and advocacy strategy entitled '10 Years of YEPP: Youth and Community Empowerment and Partnership in Practice', in order to showcase the results of 10 years of YEPP at local, regional, national and European levels. The strategy outlined the priorities for the dissemination of YEPP, while advocating for the desired changes identified by YEPP stakeholders. It also took into consideration ways to mainstream policy messages and products.

Dissemination and advocacy strategy

Drawing on the results of the evaluation of YEPP II, the '10 Years of YEPP' story has been presented using a number of communication tools to a diverse range of target audiences and key stakeholders, including the YEPP community and partners, strategic stakeholders such as foundations, politicians and EU/other institutions, including academics and practitioners and the general public.

To successfully convey the local and transnational achievements of YEPP, a number of communication tools were produced in collaboration with media experts. An important part of this campaign has been the 'Portraits of Local Programme Sites' and 'Portraits of Young People', the 'Portrait of the Transnational Dimension', the 'Portrait of Foundations' Partnership', and the 'Portrait of Partnership as a Key Concept of YEPP', all of which featured in the local and overall evaluation reports of Phase II. These portraits showcase the changes that YEPP has caused up to the end of the second phase and convey the key messages that have been summarised for policy makers (YEPP portraits).[14] Additionally, a '10 Years of YEPP' video (YEPP, 2011) illustrates the different ways in which YEPP has achieved change for young people and their communities. A number of focused dissemination and advocacy events were and will be held in order to engage with representatives of relevant target audiences at all levels, in particular at the European level.

The achievements

YEPP has created many positive achievements and this section provides but a brief summary. More details can be found in Chapter Seven, which provides number of conclusions, and in the portraits (posted on YEPP-Community.org) and in the latest evaluation report on partnership (Hasibovic, 2011). There will also be a full evaluation of the YEPP II data when the reports of the evaluation facilitators have been finalised.

Summarising the achievements, it can be said that the qualitative and quantitative growth of the Programme and the results of the external and internal evaluation of Phase I, as well as of the participatory monitoring and evaluation of YEPP II as presented in the portraits mentioned above, provide significant evidence that the overall goals of promoting civic engagement in order to bring about change and social inclusion have been largely achieved.

Quantitative growth

YEPP started in 2001 with five local sites in five European countries. At the end of the second phase, YEPP has been active in 18 Local Programme Sites in eight European countries and there is already further interest from communities in Italy to join YEPP.

Youth and community empowerment

The evaluated outcomes of YEPP indicate that significant and sustainable changes in youth and community empowerment, cross-sectoral partnership, youth policies and youth funding have been achieved in the participating Local Programme Sites during the 10 years of the programme. Within the conceptual framework of the YEPP approach to youth and community empowerment, each programme site addressed different challenges, met different needs and mobilized different resources. Each local site developed its own operational plans, with specific objectives and actions. Within this framework, a great variety and diversity of best practices emerged that led to changes that can be assessed as being caused by YEPP.

As members of the Local Support Groups, young people had opportunities to engage in local decision-making processes in partnership with other committed residents and local stakeholders and to initiate projects with their peers for their peers and for their communities. The programme opened new opportunities to allow young people's voices to be heard, extending from transnational workshops and training on youth participation and advocacy, to engaging in dialogue with local and European decision makers.

Partnership

Partnership has been a key concept of YEPP at local, regional, national and transnational levels and the partnerships that developed in YEPP II have been described fully by Hasibovic (2011).

- At transnational level, YEPP has developed an innovative and successful model of partnership between foundations, sharing resources and steering a long-term transnational programme and working in partnership with the programme partners, the INA and the NEF.
- At local level, partnership proved to be best promoted by the Local Support Groups. Local stakeholders became organised, built cross-sectoral partnerships and engaged in strategic planning and implementation processes to take the development of their communities into their own hands, to take the responsibility for bringing about change. This model can now be regarded as a best-practice tool for sustainable cross-sectoral partnership that includes stakeholders from local NGOs, foundations, municipalities and residents, including young people, who are united by common goals, actions and ideas.
- Some Local Support Groups established not-for-profit associations and community foundations that included YEPP in their portfolio for sustaining the way of working and the achievements. Local Support Groups also provided an opportunity for inter-generational cooperation, which was appreciated by the local stakeholders in the Local Programme Sites. Some Local Support Groups are operated entirely by young people.
- At regional and national levels, clusters of local sites are collaborating. For example, in Italy the Local Programme Sites in Liguria developed a closer collaboration at regional level. Recently, local coordinators

and evaluation facilitators established their own organisation, YEPP Italy, as a framework for professional exchange and for a stronger voice vis-à-vis the political level. It is the first legally formed national cluster of YEPP Programme Sites, which was one of the objectives of the second phase of YEPP.

- At transnational level, a core group of foundations has built a long-term partnership to provide expertise and support to YEPP. Furthermore, they have utilised the YEPP approach and methodology in other parts of their work.

- YEPP has established a pattern of partnership and learning from one another. YEPP has created a personal network among those involved and it opened up new insights and new practices. It created a feeling of being a community, a partnership that had something specific to present and to be proud of. Learning from international experiences has brought invaluable ideas and good practices that would not have been developed separately.

- The transnational exchanges that took place within the YEPP community helped to broaden participants' horizons, stimulated intercultural dialogue, strengthened participants' self-confidence and self-initiative and helped in opening up to the European idea. Engaging regularly in transnational events raised young people's awareness of racism and stimulated intercultural dialogue. Furthermore, local communities established their own means of exchange across Europe – for instance, through twinning. Novello in Langhe (Italy) is in process of twinning with Kristinestad (Finland), which is one of the well-implemented sites.

The following are some figures relating to the 10 years of YEPP transnational exchanges:

- Transnational YEPP community conferences and youth meetings involved about 800 participants.
- Capacity-building workshops and training sessions (at least two per year) involved more than 300 local stakeholders.
- EmpowerMediaNetwork media workshops and trainings and bi-lateral visits involved more than 500 young people.
- The YEPP steering committee (partner foundations and programme partners) met 45 times and had several conference calls.

Advocacy

With regard to the programme goal of advocacy, the evaluation showed that young people's voices were heard and local authorities gained in expertise and public support by consulting young people on a regular basis, putting young people's ideas and initiatives into action, respectively supporting their implementation. In some local authorities, the YEPP approach enhanced and strengthened existing youth policies by shifting the focus from providing services for young people to developing services and projects with young people run by young people.

As already mentioned, in Italy the not-for-profit association YEPP Italy was founded, also with the aim of strengthening the voice of YEPP vis-à-vis policy makers.

Overall achievement

The YEPP stakeholders have proved that the YEPP approach and methodology work, and do so in a wide variety of situations and cultures. The achievements described form the assets of the programme that have emerged after 10 years of application and effort, which the stakeholders at all levels will take forward.

The achievements have encouraged the YEPP stakeholders to continue the work at local and transnational levels and to bring the approach, the methods and the best practices to a broader audience. At the same time, they will address the remaining and future challenges, further develop the approach and sustain the innovations. The future of YEPP is described in the Epilogue.

Notes

[1] For a full portrait by Emer Dolphin, 2011, see: www.yepp-community. org/yepp/cms/index.php?option=com_content&task=view&id=401&Ite mid=350.

[2] For a full portrait by Jessica Bårdsnes-Malinen, 2011, see: www.yepp-community.org/yepp/cms/index.php?option=com_content&task=view&i d=403&Itemid=352.

[3] The Liffey is the main river that flows through Dublin in Ireland.

[4] For a full portrait by Tuzla Community Foundation staff members, 2011, see: www.yepp-community.org/yepp/cms/index.php?option=com_conten t&task=view&id=441&Itemid=384.

[5] 10 Years of YEPP Policy Folder (2011) 'Tuzla: Citizens drive bottom-up change in a recovering society', Berlin:YEPP International Resource Centre, International Academy. Accessible at www.yepp-community.org (10 Years of YEPP/Portraits of Local Sites).

[6] Based on the full portrait by Marjolein Delvou, 2011. See: www.yepp-community.org/yepp/cms/index.php?option=com_content&task=view&id=440&Itemid=383.

[7] Based on the full portrait by Angela Lostia, 2011. See: www.yepp-community.org/yepp/cms/index.php?option=com_content&task=view&id=428&Itemid=372.

[8] Based on the full portrait of Langhe by Silvia Maria Manfredi and Massimo Infunti, 2011. See: www.yepp-community.org/yepp/cms/index.php?option=com_content&task=view&id=426&Itemid=371.

[9] Based on the full portrait of Genoa-Cornigliano by Claudia Lanteri and Ferdinando Barcellona, 2011. See: www.yepp-community.org/yepp/cms/index.php?option=com_content&task=view&id=402&Itemid=351.

[10] Based on the full portrait of Loano by Ortensia Romano, 2011. See: www.yepp-community.org/yepp/cms/index.php?option=com_content&task=view&id=439&Itemid=382.

[11] For a full portrait by Birgit Beltle, 2011, see: www.yepp-community.org/yepp/cms/index.php?option=com_content&task=view&id=444&Itemid=387.

[12] www.yepp-community.org/yepp/cms/index.php?option=com_content&task=view&id=444&Itemid=387.

[13] For a full portrait by Katarina Šiňanská, 2011, see: www.yepp-community.org/yepp/cms/index.php?option=com_content&task=view&id=443&Itemid=386.

[14] All portraits are published at: www.yepp-community.org/yepp/cms/index.php?option=com_content&task=view&id=397&Itemid=345.

SEVEN

YEPP I and II: conclusions and policy implications

Conclusions

Youth and community empowerment

Based on the results of the evaluations carried out on both YEPP I and II, the principal conclusion to be drawn is that young people participate actively in creating sustainable change if opportunities for civic and community engagement are open to them.

Within YEPP, young people have demonstrated that they are ready for civic and community engagement and for becoming agents of change when they get the opportunity to participate in decision-making processes and when they get the opportunity to further develop their capacities and gain skills to make their voices heard. Within YEPP, young people have seized the opportunity to engage in dialogue with local, regional and European decision makers, despite their broad discontent and distrust in politics. However, as soon as politicians and administrators become serious about listening to the young people and supportive with regard to their projects, a fruitful dialogue has developed. The YEPP experience has shown that local politicians are open to engaging in dialogue with young people at local and transnational levels and to having an exchange about policies and pathways of collaboration.

Although, over the long term, it was difficult to reach and involve the most marginalised young people facing serious educational and social challenges, those who could be reached have grown gradually into active citizenship when trusted and supported, and have benefited greatly from incremental participation.

The YEPP experience has shown that ownership of local activities by young people leads to a wealth of initiatives and projects both with and for their peers and communities that can be turned into permanent structures shaping the future of the community. Examples of such initiatives that have become formalised in structures such as youth councils, youth parliaments, 'little' parliaments involving primary school children, youth television and radio channels, and youth banks.

The YEPP experience has shown that local stakeholders, including young people, seize the opportunity to engage in a complex, systematic and continuous strategic planning, implementation and evaluation process in order to bring about change in their communities if the need for change is strongly perceived and the motivation is high to engage in bringing it about.

Participatory planning and evaluation have brought fragmented local actors together and created a framework for sustainable cooperation. In particular, the participatory monitoring and evaluation process has helped local stakeholders to take ownership of the change process, although it took longer to realise the potential of such an approach. Another necessity was for them to receive reliable support and encouragement.

Furthermore, local stakeholders have taken the opportunity to enter into a close cooperation and learning process with communities in other countries. They have committed themselves to tackling youth-related issues with young people and to creating a new world of opportunities. They have been prepared to provide funds and to be at the disposal of young people to help them create and run their own initiatives and projects, for example, through youth banks and youth and community funds. They have engaged in building cross-sectoral, inter-generational partnerships in informal action groups – the Local Support Groups – or in formal organisations such as NGOs or community foundations.

The experience of YEPP has shown that keeping an active core of young people involved over a period of several years enables the more experienced ones to develop skills, allowing them to coach younger peers. This process is one of the key ingredients of long-term successful youth empowerment.

Common ground – diversity

Within the conceptual framework of YEPP, each Local Programme Site addressed its particular challenges, met its particular needs and mobilized its particular resources. Each Local Programme Site developed its own operational plans with specific objectives and actions. Within this framework, a great variety and diversity of best practices emerged. Although it turned out that several challenges were the same in several sites, the different histories of the challenges, the different cultures and ways of approaching problems made each Local Programme Site unique.

The development of a common ground, on the one hand, and respect for the cultural and social diversity and heterogeneity of the partners, on the other, have turned out to be great strengths of the YEPP approach. Local communities' need for change has been transformed into awareness, joint strategic planning, implementation and evaluation, responsibility and sustainable improvements. The YEPP Concept of Change and the multi-level approach – the innovative way of working – have been implemented through common operational tools and structures that have been flexible enough to allow each local site to adapt the YEPP approach to local needs and contexts so as to achieve the most amount of benefit and added value for the particular community.

Integration of the work at local and transnational levels

The systematic integration of the work at local and transnational levels has been one of the innovative elements of YEPP and turned out to be another strength and important ingredient for the success of the programme.

With the YEPP Programme Team including three to four full-time staff over the 10 years, a continuous and reliable support structure was established at transnational level that married together the diverse and geographically scattered local and pan-European dimensions of YEPP. In cooperation with some members of the international steering committee and some local key actors, the team was the brain behind the YEPP approach and methodology and its continuous refinement. Through regular site visits and other forms of communication, the team supported the implementation and evaluation of the YEPP Concept of Change in the different circumstances and contexts. It provided supportive material such as manuals and handbooks, and coached the local teams. Knowing each local site and most of the local actors personally, the team was able to provide consultancy and needs-based learning opportunities across the network, as well as to transfer information about examples of best practice. The team designed, organised and raised additional funds for regular transnational events – from theme-based workshops and training events to YEPP community conferences and youth meetings, which have been an inspirational and motivational dimension for the work at local level. The work at transnational level provided a successful vehicle for sharing experience and knowledge, for learning from each other, and for capacity building.

The evaluation of the partnership model of YEPP observed that:

the multilevel nature of partnership, especially its transnational element, has been very important for the overall success of partnership at all sites. The continuous support by the Programme Team ..., especially the regular visits at the local level contributed significantly to the evolution of partnership at many sites. The presence of international, high-profile actors was in some cases decisive in convincing hesitant local stakeholders (especially in the public sector) to join or support YEPP. (Hasibovic, 2011, p 52)

It can be concluded that, in the current international age, young people, including disadvantaged young people, can benefit greatly from international experience. They can learn from each other and truly benefit from these meetings, leading to a better understanding of communicating with 'foreigners'. Furthermore, they can implement what they are learning in their own communities and can share the results with their peers at other transnational meetings. The transnational events have turned out to be incentives for young people to engage locally, because this means that they have the possibility of going to other places in Europe, meeting peers from other cities and working together on common projects.

The transnational work has created a European identity for local projects that has given legitimacy and status to local activities. It has opened doors and attracted new people to the local process. Being part of a European programme helped young people to be heard by their local administration. Many of the local municipalities involved in YEPP were particularly attracted by this dimension. It created a long-term personal network among those involved and it opened up new insights and new practices and helped to develop new models of local decision making on youth empowerment and participation. It created a feeling of being a community, a partnership that had something specific to present and to be proud of that contributed significantly to the success of the programme.

Partnership

From the very beginning, partnership has been at the heart of the YEPP design and practice, including in both the transnational and the local dimensions of YEPP. The results of an evaluation of partnership as a key concept of YEPP (Hasibovic, 2011) and the results of an assessment of the foundations' partnership (*10 Years of YEPP Policy*

Folder: YEPP as a partnership of foundations, 2011) provide evidence that the development of an integrated and holistic approach based on cross-sectoral partnerships was key to sustaining change at a local level and to achieving the overall programme goals at all levels. Being involved in a partnership has enabled foundations, municipalities and others to work on a larger scale and invest in longer-term programmes than they would have done if operating alone.

One aspect of the success of YEPP was that it developed an innovative model of partnership between foundations, sharing expertise, experience and funding, as well as steering a long-term transnational programme and working in partnership with the programme partners INAgGmbH, OECD/CERI and NEF. 'Pooling of funds is positive, but even more important is the meeting of ideas and experiences, networks and contacts to create something bigger than its single parts' (*10 Years of YEPP Policy Folder: YEPP as a partnership of foundations*, 2011, p 1).

Another aspect of YEPP's success was the innovative local partnership model in the form of the Local Support Group.

The evaluation of partnership as a key concept of YEPP at the local level points out that the YEPP approach and methodology, 'especially the Cycle of Change model with its process-based approach, has proved a very useful tool for the facilitation of partnership as such ... the time and resources invested in the process are absolutely essential for building sustainable partnerships, and not a luxury' (Hasibovic, 2011, p 50).

Building, maintaining and enhancing partnerships all require a consistent coordination and imply a constant fine-tuning of common strategies and actions:

> The institutional architecture of YEPP at the local level consisting of a local coordinator, an evaluation facilitator and the Local Support Group, has proved eminently suitable for a systematic and coordinated approach to the demanding task of building and developing genuine partnerships. Yet, the role of the local coordinator stands out: By actively balancing differences in the network, by establishing links between organisations, connecting people, mediating in conflict situations, and translating complex concepts to and among network members, local coordinators are the key pillars of partnership. Therefore, there is hardly a more important personnel decision within the entire programme. (Hasibovic, 2011, p 50)

The involvement of the independent and public sectors in the partnership is of critical importance. A strategic partnership with engaged foundations, for example, provides the possibility of longer-term funding commitment:

> based on a stronger than usual involvement of the foundations in the operational activities and strategic planning. The hands-on approach of the Compagnia di San Paolo in Turin-Mirafiori has contributed significantly, perhaps even decisively, to the establishment of a Community Foundation in this district, and might, therefore, be considered a best-practice approach to donor–beneficiary partnerships. (Hasibovic, 2011, p 51)

The involvement of the public sector (the local political and administrative institutions and services) as early as possible 'is not just a strategic option, but an essential pillar of the partnership' (Hasibovic, 2011, p 51). An early formal agreement signed by all stakeholder groups has proved to be a useful instrument for establishing a successful cross-sectoral partnership.

Equality, trust, openness and good leadership are the essential ingredients of effective and successful partnerships. For example, it turned out to be a crucial element of the innovative model of the partnership of foundations that the big, powerful foundations worked together with smaller foundations on an equal basis. This way of working together was recognised by all partners as mutually beneficial.

At the local level, the evaluation of the partnership came to the conclusion that:

> the intense, longstanding and regular collaboration in the Local Support Groups has offered unique opportunities to get to know each other and build trust, which has opened new channels of transferability of trust within and outside the network. The Local Support Group model is an institutional innovation which can certainly be considered a best-practice model for partnership-based programmes … While being very important, interpersonal trust alone is not sufficient and must be complemented by a reasonable level of inter-organizational trust. In this way, partnerships remain more stable and less vulnerable to changes in key personnel and LSG members. (Hasibovic, 2011, p 52)

It was observed that the YEPP model of partnership had a strong participatory and, therefore, democratising effect at local level. Furthermore, partnership has also been functioning at regional and national levels, where clusters of sites have been collaborating.

Finally, the conclusion from all levels of YEPP is that partnership is cost-effective. By joining resources and creating synergies, avoiding duplication of activities and not inventing the wheel again, partnership saves money.

Nevertheless, some of the partner foundations had difficulty in continuing to make the stipulated financial contribution over the 10-year period, especially against the background of the financial crisis that started in late 2008, which made a reduction of about 30% in the grant giving of some foundations inevitable. A conclusion drawn from this experience is that the challenge for future work will be to strengthen existing partnerships and at the same time to identify a differentiated system of diverse partnerships, keeping in mind that partnership, as a key concept of YEPP, is an essential pillar of the success of the approach. In terms of funding, possibilities for income generation also need to be looked at.

In this regard, it would have been helpful if the private sector had been more forthcoming, since businesses can provide many different types of support – from work experience to direct financial input. Although several attempts were made to involve the corporate sector, at both local and transnational levels, only a few initiatives came to fruition.

Committed people and institutions

The development of YEPP over the 10 years was made possible by the strong commitment of all YEPP stakeholder groups – the foundations, municipalities, local coordinators, evaluation facilitators, Local Support Group members and the many young people, as well as the Italian support team and the YEPP Programme Team. They made the significant and sustainable changes in the local communities possible, and made the regional and transnational network of YEPP a lively and beneficial platform.

The partner foundations' unwavering support over 10 years, and additional funding from the European Commission, Youth in Action Programme and other funders, including local/regional foundations and municipalities, made it possible for YEPP to develop and practise its approach and methodology and brought about sustainable change in a number of communities. Such a reliable basis and network is crucial for success.

Funding

Finally, it can be concluded that long-term change processes need to be based on longer-term reliable resources and the voluntary commitment of local stakeholders. Implementing the YEPP approach and methodology has required substantial investment in ways of providing funds as well as voluntary capacities. While in most Local Programme Sites the part-time positions of the local coordinator and evaluation facilitator were finally provided by the municipalities, the Local Support Groups were based on voluntary work by local stakeholders, including young people; and funds for activities were often provided by foundations, the European Commission and other sponsors. At the same time, the public and independent sectors' approach of joining forces in a partnership model was highly cost-effective, as explained in preceding sections.

General conclusions

At the end of YEPP II, the conclusion from YEPP I that the programme worked and created sustainable change in communities when its approach and methodology were well implemented was clearly confirmed, in particular in the cases of the new Local Programme Sites in Italy. Local Programme Sites that managed the full implementation demonstrated the greatest effects and outcomes in terms of the overall goals of YEPP. A reflective, hands-on approach with tangible results – guided by theory and the results of research in the field and by transfer of knowledge, and supported by capacity building – helped local stakeholders, in particular young people, to engage in a long-term structural change process.

The basic idea of YEPP, to embed youth empowerment in community empowerment, worked. It was a significant ingredient for bringing about sustainable change and for impacting on the environment in which young people develop. It is most unlikely that a singular youth project would have achieved what became possible with a holistic youth and community development process. Bottom-up mobilisation of citizens – among them young people – is particularly effective for empowering disadvantaged communities.

Although there were significant differences between the communities in which YEPP worked, they also had a number of factors in common. Nearly all communities had the problems of:

- a lack of access by young people to decision-making processes;
- young people's mobility;
- spaces for young people – and also spaces for citizens – in the form of youth and community centres;
- access to services and learning opportunities; and
- the integration of a large number of workers from within the country,[1] from other European countries and from other continents.

Altogether, the local stakeholders in these communities were in need of a model to tackle these challenges and to overcome fragmentation and social exclusion.

In almost all cases, YEPP was able to provide an approach and methodology to address these challenges and to develop answers in partnership-based joint efforts. Thus, it can be concluded that YEPP has created a model for inclusion, active participation and civic engagement that will work for most communities and young people where there is a need to bring about sustainable change in order to overcome marginalising processes and disadvantage.

It can be concluded that YEPP II represents a tried and tested multi-dimensional, multi-level, intercultural and cross-sectoral approach to and methodology for youth empowerment and community development that has grown out of the original concept YEPP I and could now almost be described as an 'industry standard'. It is very much appreciated by the stakeholders, and uses an effective approach and methodology to offer increased opportunities to those living in disadvantaged communities, through a process of youth and community empowerment.

However, despite many positive outcomes, YEPP still faces many challenges that need to be addressed as a priority. These challenges are closely interlinked and include the need for:

- increased efforts to reach the most marginalised young people;
- a reduction in the growing youth unemployment and child and youth poverty; and
- the building of truly cross-sectoral partnerships that will include the private sector.

Transferring skills from voluntary projects to the more general labour market, as well as supporting entrepreneurship, requires close cooperation with the local and transnational business sectors. Young people facing serious educational and social challenges are hard to reach and to involve in a sustainable manner, but can benefit greatly from incremental participation.

A growing number of disadvantaged young people

The consequences of the global financial crisis, and also of the failures of political systems in terms of the further alienation of significant groups of young people in society, have created a new dimension of marginalisation and worldwide 'outpourings of discontent ... and global unrest' (Mason, 2012, p 6) and the question of who are now 'the disadvantaged' must be asked.

Youth movements and protests, as well as the popular drive for democracy and self-determination in North African countries, the so-called Arab Spring, need to be understood as new challenges and responded to with new initiatives. Mason observes that:

> at the centre of all the protest movements is a new sociological type: the graduate with no future. In North Africa there is a demographic bulge of young people, including graduates and students, who are unable to get a decent job – or indeed any job. By 2011, there was 20% youth unemployment across the region, where two-thirds of the population is under the age of 30. In Libya, despite high GDP growth, youth unemployment stood at 30%. But youth unemployment is not a factor confined to North Africa. In Spain, in 2011 youth unemployment was running at 46%, a figure partially ameliorated by the tendency for young Spaniards to live off their extended families. In Britain, on the eve of the student riots of 2010, youth unemployment stood at 20%. (Mason, 2012, p 8)

There is now a new factor that needs to be considered in any youth and community empowerment activity: the role and the potential of the social media and new technology. Mason further observes that:

> social media and new technology were crucial in shaping the revolutions of 2011, just as they shaped industry, finance and mass culture in the preceding decade. What's important is not that the Egyptian youth used Facebook, or that the British students used Twitter and the Greek rioters organised via Indymedia, but what they used these media for – and

what such technology does to hierarchies, ideas and actions.
(Mason, 2012, p 9)

A programme, like YEPP, that has come to stand for the civic
engagement of young people to participate actively in decision-making
processes and to shape their communities is ideally positioned to
contribute to the prevention of further processes of alienation and to
work with young people and the local, global and virtual communities
in which they live. It can harness young people's energy for change
and help to transform the strong motivation underlying the current
movements from confrontation to participation and the strengthening
of civil society. Such tangible results would encourage social inclusion
and improve the quality of life.

Policy implications

Impact locally, nationally and internationally

Within the YEPP community, it was always a shared belief that
sustainable change needs to be anchored in long-term empowerment
processes, to be put into practice in partnership and, finally, to be
mainstreamed in local, regional, national and European policies and
structures. As a result, advocacy has been one of the core programme
goals of YEPP, but in order to draw policy implications from the
YEPP experiences, it is necessary to take the different sectors – public,
independent and private – and the different levels of policy making
–local, regional, national and European – into consideration

Various evaluations show that the YEPP approach and the examples
of best practice that have emerged have been adopted by several *local*
governments when designing their youth policies. YEPP's approach
and methodology have helped local decision makers to design youth
policies, and also to get input from young people into other policy
areas. These municipalities have been prepared to make personnel
available and to provide some funding for activities. To cover the whole
programme, additional funds have been raised. In other municipalities,
the approach has enhanced and strengthened existing youth policies
by shifting the focus away from providing services *for* young people
and towards developing services and projects *with* young people run
by young people.

There were further attempts to influence policies at *regional* level.
For example, in 2009 the transnational YEPP training in advocacy
strategies led to the establishment of the Regional Youth Advocacy

Group in the region of Liguria (Italy). This group organised a meeting with candidates for the presidency of the region in order to discuss the candidates' plans for future youth policies. The youth delegates from four YEPP Local Programme Sites in Liguria used this as an opportunity to present their own ideas and examples of best practice with regard to youth participation in decision-making processes and what they had achieved so far. They invited the future president to speak at the YEPP Community Conference and Youth Meeting in Genoa in October 2010. In response, the *assessore* for social policies and youth of the regional government of Liguria attended the conference and spoke at the 'Talk Show'. The dialogue has been followed up and has led to some support of youth-led activities in Liguria.

At the *national level* in Italy, it is hoped that the establishment of the association 'YEPP Italy' will strengthen the voice vis-à-vis the political level and increase the impact (see p 146). The OECD/CERI brought YEPP to the attention of its member countries at the national level through the external evaluation process and at a number of committees. At one meeting the office of the Secretary-General of the OECD offered NEF the opportunity to input the YEPP approach at one of its regular policy forums. However, this offer was not taken up – perhaps because the foundations concerned felt that YEPP was at too early a stage of development (it was still YEPP I). Unfortunately, nothing concrete emerged from the other meetings or approaches of the OECD/CERI secretariat. National approaches were also made through the YEPP network, especially in Finland and Ireland, countries which were originally very interested in the OECD/CERI work on integrated services. Nevertheless, YEPP helped to strengthen the contacts with the national government in Ireland, and YEPP was presented to the National Board of Education in Finland and, as reported in Chapter Three, a delegation from South Korea visited Kristinestad, Finland, as a result of OECD/CERI involvement, to explore the possibility of joining YEPP. Compagnia di San Paulo had some contact with the Ministry of Education in Italy, but nothing further developed. YEPP is, however, making its way up the national agenda in those countries where there are multiple YEPP Local Programme Sites.

At the *European* level, YEPP has become a member of children- and youth-focused lobby organisations and has participated in consultations of the European Commission. This is a field that needs further exploration and development.

Impact on foundations

Most of the foundations closely involved in YEPP adopted the approach and methodology for their further programming and grant giving. Some of them acquired criteria for assessing the potential quality and innovation of submitted proposals. These criteria became guidelines for their programming and grant giving. In Italy, for example, Compagnia di San Paolo designed a major new programme in Turin on the basis of the YEPP approach and methodology.

The wider policy implications of YEPP

Based on the examples of best practice from 10 years of YEPP, a discussion of the policy implications of YEPP must go beyond singular youth and/or social policy. Policies related to youth and community issues are made in almost all governmental and administrative departments, as well as by foundations. Youth and community issues are cross-cutting issues and need to be addressed across traditional policy domains. The implications outlined in the following paragraphs are addressed to policy makers in general, as well as to those shaping youth and social policies in particular.

First of all, the YEPP experiences show that cross-cutting youth and community policies should be developed in all sectors and existing policies should be reviewed in terms of participation, inclusiveness and effectiveness.

Any policy making should take young people seriously and not underestimate them, but think of them as citizens of today, not only as adults of tomorrow. Policy making should enter into a regular dialogue and be open to the civic and community engagement of young people. In order to gain invaluable expertise and public support, the design and implementation of policies should be developed in a regular, consultative process and engage citizens and, in particular, young people, in the decision-making processes. The talents and initiatives of all residents, including young people, should be recognised. Policy makers should look at young people, in particular, as *assets and resources, not as problems*. For example, public intervention and dialogue with young people and youth organisations should be broadly based and aimed not only at high-risk factors such as drug trafficking but also at new urban and rural regeneration plans.

The voices of young people should be heard and structures and tools should be provided so as to ensure that their views are actively taken into account. Local partners and municipalities should support young people in making a difference. They can provide creative and sustainable solutions in different areas of policy. Important policy implications drawn from the YEPP experience are, for example:

- Social investment funds managed by young people should be made available in order to develop young people's skills while creating improvements for the whole community.
- A culture of continuous evaluation, in particular participatory evaluation, needs to be supported through policies, for example by including it as a non-negotiable requirement in any publicly or privately supported project. YEPP showed that communities will shy away from evaluating innovations if they can, but YEPP also demonstrated the clear value of feedback for improving those same innovations.
- Policies should include the strengthening of civil society, which includes the strengthening of the position of both informal and formal local actors' groups, such as the Local Support Groups, as well as community foundations. In countries with young democracies there is often a need to establish taxation laws and procedures for philanthropic giving; in other countries it often means providing support for local stakeholders to use existing possibilities.
- With regard to securing the benefits of a transnational dimension that were mentioned earlier, policies should open up to learning from other countries in Europe and beyond and to supporting a systematic and integrated approach of work at local and at transnational levels and the transfer of knowledge and experiences.
- Policies of the public and independent sector should include structures and tools to enable local stakeholders to engage in transnational exchanges on a regular basis. The European Commission has several programmes to support such a transnational dimension. It is the current policy of the Commission to promote regular exchanges, not one-off events. This policy matches well with the YEPP approach and should be used effectively by local, regional and national policies.
- One of the most important policy implications for the public sector, as well as for the independent sector, is to work in cross-sectoral partnerships including the private sector. More can be achieved when working together than when sectors work alone. Foundations and municipalities should work in partnership and in close collaboration with local stakeholders – citizens' groups and/ or civil society organisations – to bring together their collective expertise, funds and decision-making powers. Since youth and

community empowerment require long-term commitment, working in partnerships would pool funds, personnel and expertise. Foundations are often closer to civil society organisations and the citizens themselves, and can help to inspire change processes that can then be mainstreamed by the public sector. Foundations are in a good position to play a catalytic role and to become involved in capacity building and the empowerment of the local stakeholders in communities, and to help to promote transnational exchange in order to support the public sector in bringing about necessary change.

- In order to secure the obvious benefits of civic engagement of citizens, especially of young people, policy making should acknowledge voluntary work in particular and look into the possibilities for certification of voluntary work and for its recognition as a qualification and work experience.
- In order to prepare young people for civic engagement and to strengthen the voluntary sector, education policies should look into supporting pupils to engage in community services and to learn as early as possible in their lives how to participate actively. This needs to become part of the mainstream curriculum, as was done, for example, in the community school movement in the US, the UK and other European countries.
- The non-formal learning sector needs to be strengthened and acknowledged as a highly important element of life-long learning that can make a major contribution to society. Civic engagement needs to become a real thread through all walks of life, and a pillar of democracy.
- One outstanding policy implication is that all cut-backs in the area of youth- and community-related policies need to be halted. All sectors need to invest in young people; the further alienation of groups of young people must be stopped because the future of our societies is at serious risk. The priorities of current policies in a time of the global crisis need to be reviewed and decisions need to be made that will secure the potential of our youth.
- YEPP has created a different way of working and of using existing funds. It has demonstrated that change processes do not always mean providing additional public money, but often require a reorganisation of funds and the integration of innovative ideas and ways of working. Bringing the expertise, experience and commitment of citizens into close cooperation with professionals creates a rich resource for implementing needed change. Policy making should take this into consideration and be open to reviewing the usual ways of working,

to creating synergies between different resources and, if necessary, to allocating enough funding for innovation and new approaches aimed at creating lasting change.

Note
[1] For example, migration of Italian nationals from the south to the north of Italy.

Epilogue: the future of YEPP

As a major conclusion of the 10 years of YEPP, it was decided to continue the work at local level in the communities, to develop a new structure at transnational level and to bring the YEPP approach and methodology to a wider audience.

In early 2009, a broad and participative consultation process was initiated with YEPP stakeholders at local and transnational levels in order to develop a plan for the future of YEPP post-2011, when YEPP as a foundation-led programme would come to an end. The results of the consultation process were assessed by the YEPP Post-2011 Working Group, which was set up in November 2009 and included representatives of YEPP stakeholder groups.

The consultation process identified the clear wish of the majority of the local teams to continue the work in the Local Programme Sites based on the YEPP approach and methodology, as well as to continue the work at transnational level. The main issue was to identify the best structure for the work at transnational level so as to further support and promote youth and community empowerment, partnership and advocacy.

The Working Group proposed to establish the YEPP International Resource Centre (YEPP IRC) at the INAgGmbH at the Free University of Berlin, in order to support the work in accordance with the YEPP approach and methodology at local, regional, national and international levels. This proposed new structure was approved by the Local Teams at the 5th YEPP Community Conference and Youth Meeting in Görlitz-Zgorzelec (Germany-Poland) in November 2011.

The YEPP IRC was opened on 1 January 2012 at the Institute for Community Education of the International Academy.

The YEPP IRC is designed to function as:

- an international agency to support local communities involved in YEPP in achieving youth and community empowerment
- a research-based youth and community development centre to enhance and strengthen the YEPP approach and to make an impact in the field
- an advocate for youth and community empowerment at political level in order to influence youth and community related policies.

The YEPP IRC mission

The mission of the YEPP IRC is to bring about sustainable change in local communities with fewer opportunities, across Europe and beyond, in order to build an active civil society involving local stakeholders – in particular, young people.

The YEPP IRC goals and principles

The YEPP IRC is committed to five goals, which are at the heart of YEPP:

Goal 1: Youth empowerment

To enable young people who are at risk of social exclusion and/or live in areas with fewer opportunities to participate in local decision-making processes, to create change in their communities and to become active citizens in the wider society.

Goal 2: Community empowerment

To create self-confident and competent communities, so that residents and local stakeholders become active citizens and advocate changes to the environment in which children and youth develop.

Goal 3: Partnership

To establish strong and sustainable partnerships and strategic alliances involving actors from different sectors (public, private and independent) and levels (local, regional, national and international), in order to foster youth and community empowerment.

Goal 4: Advocacy

To influence public and independent policies to ensure that the principles of youth empowerment, community empowerment and partnership become mainstream and are transformed into action at all levels.

Goal 5: Learning

To provide opportunities for learning and capacity building through exchange and transfer of knowledge and expertise at local, regional, national and international levels.

The YEPP IRC is committed to seven principles that express the essence of YEPP's approach and underpin the diverse activities and structures at local, regional, national and international levels:

Principle 1: Local partnerships

Local stakeholders establish cross-sectoral collaboration, joint action and strategic alliances in informal action groups or formal organisations.

Principle 2: Young people as main actors of local changes

Young people participate actively in the decision-making process and have decision-making power.

Principle 3: Equal opportunities

Equal opportunities are promoted regardless of racial or ethnic origin, education, gender, age, disability, sexual orientation, religion or belief.

Principle 4: Participatory strategic planning

Local stakeholders – including young people – engage in joint strategic planning based on the YEPP Concept of Change and the Participatory YEPP Monitoring and Evaluation concept, leading to recurrent systematic processes of analysis, planning, implementation and evaluation.

Principle 5: Transnational partnerships

YEPP sites establish transnational partnerships and are supported by an international resource centre.

Principle 6: Transnational exchanges

At the transnational level, local stakeholders engage in peer exchanges and learning, in training sessions and capacity building, in networking and in building strategic alliances.

Principle 7: Influencing policies

YEPP expands its approach and methodology to a broader field of practitioners and decision makers, so as to be able to influence public and independent policies at all levels. In order to achieve its mission and overall goals, the YEPP IRC will sustain, scale up, strengthen and disseminate the YEPP approach and methodology, as well as expand the YEPP network. It will continue to transform local communities' perceived need for change into awareness, joint strategic planning, implementation and evaluation, responsibility and sustainable improvements. The YEPP IRC will promote the implementation of the YEPP Concept of Change, as outlined in the YEPP Manifesto, and the multi-level approach through common operational tools and structures, which are flexible enough to allow each local site to adapt the YEPP approach to the local needs and contexts. The YEPP IRC engages in expanding YEPP, reaching more communities across Europe and beyond.

Figure 4: The YEPP IRC areas of work

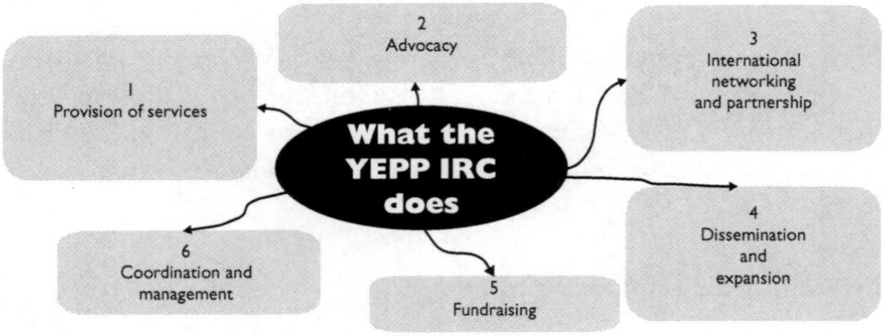

Provision of services

The IRC provides needs-based methodological support to a range of stakeholders in local communities in order to implement the YEPP Concept of Change and its principles as outlined in the YEPP Manifesto so as to achieve the overall YEPP goals and the mission of the IRC. For example, the remaining challenges, as identified at the end of YEPP II, will have high priority in the IRC's work in support of the work in the YEPP sites.

Support is provided to existing local YEPP sites (Local Programme Sites in the previous phases of YEPP) as well as to communities that will adopt the YEPP approach.

This support will be provided by the IRC Team in cooperation with members of the steering committee, members of the local teams and local, regional or national YEPP organisations. The support is intended for multiple stakeholders participating at community and international level, through different tools and activities, including, for example:

- regular site visits and consultation and coaching on the ground;
- manuals and handbooks for local coordinators, evaluation facilitators, local support groups, and young people addressing key issues of the YEPP approach, as well as key challenges;
- theme-based international capacity building and training; local and international media workshops and exchanges of the EmpowerMediaNetwork and so on.

Advocacy

The YEPP IRC will advocate for civic engagement and participation and strive to influence policies at local, regional, national and international levels. This includes making the voice of the IRC and the whole YEPP network heard on political issues regarding youth, through different channels – for example, through participation in consultation events of the European Commission, publications in relevant media, holding events with policy makers.

The YEPP IRC supports the participating communities and local teams in strengthening the links to local politicians and authorities.

International networking and partnership

The YEPP IRC will facilitate the YEPP International Network and coordinate platforms for international exchange and learning, including an effective use of media. The YEPP IRC will act as a focal point for an active international network and organise international conferences and youth meetings, capacity-building workshops, training, thematic youth exchanges and media workshops of the EmpowerMediaNetwork.

The IRC will strive to establish international partnerships. Tasks include presentations at international events and organising events that target specific audiences so as to further build an expert reputation and reach out to make connections in and beyond Europe.

Dissemination and expansion

The YEPP IRC will disseminate and promote the YEPP approach through different channels both across Europe and beyond. The dissemination approach will include the effective use of the internet. The IRC will strive to reach more communities in order to broaden its basis and network so as to have a stronger voice and impact on policies. Communities can become involved in different ways, according to their own needs and conditions, as long as they work in accordance to the YEPP Manifesto.

Fundraising

The YEPP IRC will engage in fundraising and income generation in order to build a sustainable basis for the IRC infrastructure and for operational activities. Furthermore, it will provide support for stakeholders at all levels so as to raise funds for the implementation of activities and to further sustain achievements.

Coordination and management

The coordination and management ensures that the mission and the goals are achieved and the principles are respected. This includes: development and implementation of the Strategic Plan, including a Business Plan with strategies for fundraising and income generation, an Activity Plan and an Evaluation Plan for regular monitoring and improvement of the IRC's performance; presentation of a budget and ensuring that accepted financial practices are adhered to; coordination of the governance structure; meeting the accountability requirements.

Participating local communities

Participating local communities (through the various stakeholders in those communities) will work in accordance with the YEPP Manifesto, which outlines the approach and methodology of YEPP. These communities are linked with the YEPP IRC through a Memorandum of Understanding.

Governance

The INAgGmbH, as a non-for-profit limited company under German law, provides the legal framework, employs the staff members and hosts the YEPP IRC at its premises at the Free University of Berlin. Within INA, the IRC is located in the Institute for Community Education, which provides professional support.

Guidance on the YEPP IRC's strategy is provided by an established steering committee that reflects the diversity of the YEPP Post-2011 Working Group, with representatives of YEPP stakeholder groups, including foundations, local coordinators, evaluation facilitators, young people, EmpowerMediaNetwork (EMN) Coordinator and INA.

Staff and consultants

At the operational level, the YEPP IRC Team includes a director, deputy director and an administrator/event manager/organiser to share the tasks supported by consultants with long-standing YEPP experience and/or fundraising expertise.

Funding

The establishment of the YEPP IRC will be facilitated by start-up funding for 2012 from a group of foundations and municipalities, possibly also for 2013.

In order to sustain the YEPP IRC, the Business Plan relates to fundraising as well as income-generation strategies. Different audiences need to be approached.

Finally

The authors hope that the work on youth and community empowerment that has been reported and discussed in this book will stimulate in the reader an interest in YEPP and its approach and methodology and in the best practices and experiences in the communities that have been involved. The YEPP community and the YEPP IRC staff will be happy to respond to any enquiries. They all intend to work towards expanding the network in order to make a greater impact on policies, so as to achieve sustainable change in our communities.

References

10 Years of YEPP Policy Folder (2011) *Genoa-Cornigliano: Modern identity and social cohesion in a post-industrial area*, Berlin: YEPP International Resource Centre, International Academy. Accessible at www.yepp-community.org (10 Years of YEPP/Portraits of Local Sites).

10 Years of YEPP Policy Folder (2011) *Görlitz/Zgorzelec: Building new bridges in a cross-border community*, Berlin: YEPP International Resource Centre, International Academy. Accessible at www.yepp-community.org (10 Years of YEPP/Portraits of Local Sites).

10 Years of YEPP Policy Folder (2011) *Kecerovce-Olšava: Breaking down the barriers of social exclusion of Roma*, Berlin: YEPP International Resource Centre, International Academy. Accessible at www.yepp-community.org (10 Years of YEPP/Portraits of Local Sites).

10 Years of YEPP Policy Folder (2011) *Langhe: Partnership of municipalities broadens young people's horizons*, Berlin: YEPP International Resource Centre, International Academy. Accessible at www.yepp-community.org (10 Years of YEPP/Portraits of Local Sites).

10 Years of YEPP Policy Folder (2011) *Loano: Young people as autonomous agents of change*, Berlin: YEPP International Resource Centre, International Academy. Accessible at www.yepp-community.org (10 Years of YEPP/Portraits of Local Sites).

10 Years of YEPP Policy Folder (2011) *YEPP as a partnership of foundations*, Berlin: YEPP International Resource Centre, International Academy. Accessible at www.yepp-community.org (10 Years of YEPP/ YEPP Transnational).

Aassve, A., Iacovou, M. and Letizia, M. (2006) 'Youth poverty and transition to adulthood in Europe', *Demographic Research*, vol 15, pp 21–50.

Annie E. Casey Foundation (1997) 'Message from Chairman', *Annie E. Casey Foundation: 1998–99 Annual Report*, in P. Bleckmann and A. Krüger, *Youth Empowerment Partnership Programme – final cross-cutting report of the internal evaluation*, Berlin: International Academy. Accessible at www.yepp-community.org (10 Years of YEPP/YEPP Phase I).

Annie E. Casey (2010) *Making Connections*, http://www.aecf.org/ OurWork/CommunityChange.aspx.

Bårdsnes-Malinen, J. (2011) *Portrait of Kristinestad 2002–2010*. Accessible at www.yepp-community.org (10 Years of YEPP/Portraits of Local Sites).

Becker, D. and Weyermann, B. (2006) *Gender, conflict transformation and the psychosocial approach*. Toolkit. Edited by the Swiss Agency for Development and Cooperation, in P. Bleckmann and A. Krüger *Youth Empowerment Partnership Programme – final cross-cutting report of the internal evaluation*, Berlin: International Academy. Accessible at www.yepp-community.org (10 Years of YEPP/YEPP Phase I).

Beltle, B. (2011) *Görlitz/Zgorzelec (Germany-Poland). The portrait*. Accessible at www.yepp-community.org (10 Years of YEPP/Portraits of Local Sites).

Bleckmann, P. (2004) *Youth and community empowerment through cultural activities*, Brussels/Berlin: Network of European Foundations for Innovative Cooperation and YEPP.

Bleckmann, P., Krüger, A. and Sischka, K. (2005) *What works? What does not? Analysis of the programme development to date in the light of YEPP's theory and concept of change*. Interim assessment report (final version), implementation phase until June 2005. YEPP internal evaluation, Berlin: International Academy.

Bleckmann, P. and Krüger, A. (2007) *Youth Empowerment Partnership Programme – final cross-cutting report of the internal evaluation*, Berlin: International Academy. Accessible at www.yepp-community.org (10 Years of YEPP/YEPP Phase I).

Bleckmann, P., Eaton, L. and Krüger, A. (2007) *Youth and community empowerment in practice. Practitioners' handbook based on the concept and the experiences of the Youth Empowerment Partnership Programme*, Berlin: YEPP International Resource Centre, International Academy.

Brossa, I. (2010) *Portrait of the youth network Porta Palazzo 'The Gate'*. Accessible at www.yepp-community.org (10 Years of YEPP/Portraits of Local Sites).

Business for Social Responsibility (2007), in P. Bleckmann and A. Krüger (2007) *Youth Empowerment Partnership Programme – final cross-cutting report of the internal evaluation*, Berlin: International Academy. Accessible at www.yepp-community.org (10 Years of YEPP/YEPP Phase I).

Colley, H., Hoskins, B., Parveva, T. and Boetzelen, P. (2005) *Social inclusion and young people*. Report of a research seminar, 31 October–2 November, 2005. The Council of Europe and European Commission, Youth Research Partnership (eds), in P. Bleckmann and A. Krüger *Youth Empowerment Partnership Programme – final cross-cutting report of the internal evaluation*, Berlin: International Academy. Accessible at www.yepp-community.org (10 Years of YEPP/YEPP Phase I).

Council of Europe and European Commission Youth Research Partnership (2005) *The 'E&C' in Germany ('Development and opportunities for young people in disadvantaged neighbourhoods')*. Accessible at: http://www.berlinprocess.eundc.de/index.html

Dayton Peace Agreement on Bosnia and Herzegovina (1995), www1.umn.edu/humanrts/icty/dayton/daytonsum.html.

Dewey, J. (1899–1924: 1921–1922), in J. Boydston (ed.) *The middle works of John Dewey, essays on philosophy, education, and the Orient*, vol 13, Carbondale, IL: Southern Illinois University Press.

Dolphin, Emer (2011) *Dublin North-East Inner City (Ireland). The portrait.* Accessible at www.yepp-community.org (10 Years of YEPP/Portraits of Local Sites).

Engelhardt-Wendt, E., Krüger, A., Leupold, S. and Strocka, C. (2008) *Participatory output monitoring (POM). Manual for monitoring teams*, Berlin: YEPP International Resource Centre, International Academy (INA).

Engelhardt-Wendt, E. Krüger, A. Leupold, S. and Strocka, C. (2009) *Participatory output monitoring (POM). Manual for monitoring teams* (2nd edn), Berlin: YEPP International Resource Centre, International Academy (INA).

Evans, P., Bronheim, S., Bynner, J., Klasen, S., Magrab, P. and Ranson, S. (2000) 'Social exclusion and children – creating identity capital: some conceptual issues and practical solutions', in G. Walraven, C. Parsons, D. van Veen and C. Day (eds) *Combating Social Exclusion Through Education: Laissez-faire, Authoritarianism or Third Way?*, Antwerpen/Apeldoorn: Garant.

Friedman, J. (1992) *Empowerment: The politics of alternative development*, Cambridge, MA: Blackwell.

Hasibovic, S. (2011) *Partnership as a key concept of the Youth Empowerment Partnership Programme: Achievements and lessons learnt. Evaluation report*, Berlin: YEPP International Resource Centre, International Academy. Accessible at www.yepp-community.org (10 Years of YEPP/YEPP Transnational).

Henderson, P. and Vercseg, I. (2010) *Community development and civil society. Making connections in the European context*, Bristol: The Policy Press.

Institute for Interdisciplinary Research on Conflict and Violence (IKG) at the University Bielefeld (2002–2005) *Disintegration processes – strengthening the integration potentials of modern society*, www.uni-bielefeld.de/ikg/eng/project_strengthening-integration.htm.

International Youth Foundation (2007) 'The positive youth development approach', in P. Bleckmann and A. Krüger *Youth Empowerment Partnership Programme – final cross-cutting report of the internal evaluation*, Berlin: International Academy. Accessible at www. yepp-community.org (10 Years of YEPP/YEPP Phase I).

Katsbert, T. and Strocka, C. (2010) *YEPP overall interim evaluation report 2009*, Berlin: YEPP International Resource Centre, International Academy.

Krüger, A. (1997) 'Urban regeneration and residents' involvement – developments in Germany over the last two decades', in P. Henderson, (ed.) *'No Europe without us' – setting the scene: Community-based responses to urban deprivation in five European countries*, The Hague: LSA and Combined European Bureau for Social Development.

Krüger, A. (2002) *Youth empowerment within the context of YEPP*, Berlin: YEPP International Resource Centre, International Academy.

Krüger, A. and Picht, R. (1999) *Youth and youth policies in the United States. Working paper one: Integrating youth into a changing society. The role of foundations and corporate funders*, Brussels: European Foundation Centre.

Krüger, A. and Zimmer, J. (2001) *Die Ausbildung der Erzieherinnen neu erfinden*. Neuwied: Luchterhand.

Krüger, A., Leupold, S. and Strocka, C. (2008) *Evaluation design and implementation plan for YEPP Phase II*. Presented to the YEPP steering committee at the EFC Conference in Istanbul, 29 May 2008, Berlin: YEPP International Resource Centre, International Academy (INA).

Krüger, A., Leupold, S., Strocka, C. and Duke, P. (2009) *The YEPP practitioners handbook. Youth and community empowerment in practice* (2nd edn), Berlin: YEPP International Resource Centre, International Academy.

Leat, D. (2005) *Theories for social change*. International Network on Strategic Philanthropy and the Bertelsmann Stiftung, in P. Bleckmann and A. Krüger *Youth Empowerment Partnership Programme – final cross-cutting report of the internal evaluation*, Berlin: International Academy. Accessible at www.yepp-community.org (10 Years of YEPP/YEPP Phase I).

Lewis, D. (1973) 'Causation', *The Journal of Philosophy*, vol 70, no 17, pp, 556–67.

McCawley, P.F. (undated) *The logic model for program planning and evaluation*, University of Idaho – Extension. CIS 1097, www.uiweb. uidaho.edu/extension/LogicModel.pdf.

Mason, P. (2012) *Why it's kicking off everywhere: The new global revolution*, London and New York: Verso.

OECD (1995) *Our children and families at risk*, Paris: OECD.

OECD (1998) *Co-ordinating services for our children and families at risk – a world view*, Paris: OECD.

OECD/CERI (2007) *Promoting partnerships for inclusion. Final report of the external evaluation and foundation partnership for the Youth Empowerment Partnership Programme (YEPP)*, Paris: OECD. Accessible at www.yepp-community.org (10 Years of YEPP/YEPP Phase I).

Owen, R. (1813) *A new view of society: Essays on the formation of human character*, London: Cadell & Davies.

Pike, M. (2003) *Can do citizens: Re-building marginalised communities*, London: Social Enterprises Services.

QSR International (2002) *N6 (NUD*IST)*, accessed at: http://www.qsrinternational.com.

Reese, W.S., Thorup, C.L. and Gerson, T.K. (2002) *What works in public/private partnering: Building alliances for youth development*, Baltimore, MD: International Youth Foundation, www.iyfnet.org.

Robson, C. (2011) *Real world research*, Oxford: Wiley-Blackwell.

Rodenberg, B. and Wichterich, Ch. (1999) *Empowerment: A study of women's projects abroad*, Berlin: Heinrich-Böll Foundation.

Scarman Trust (2007) *Asset-based community development (ABCD)*, in P. Bleckmann and A. Krüger *Youth Empowerment Partnership Programme – final cross-cutting report of the internal evaluation*, Berlin: International Academy. Accessible at www.yepp-community.org (10 Years of YEPP/YEPP Phase I).

Sen, A. (1999) *Development as freedom*, New York: Knopf.

Senge, P.M. (1990) *The fifth discipline. The art and practice of the learning organization*, London: Random House.

Šiňanská, K. (2011) *Kecerovce (Slovakia). The portrait*. Accessible at www.yepp-community.org (10 Years of YEPP/Portraits of Local Sites).

Smith, M.K. (2001) 'Kurt Lewin, groups, experiential learning and action research', *The Encyclopedia of Informal Education*, www.infed.org/thinkers/et-lewin.htm.

Strandberg, N. (2001) *Conceptualizing empowerment as a transformative strategy for poverty eradication and the implications for measuring progress*, www.un.org/womenwatch/daw/csw/empower/documents/Strandberg-EP6.pdf.

Strocka, C., Duke, P., Engelhardt-Wendt, E., Krüger, A. and Leupold, S. (2008) *Manual for evaluation facilitators, Part 1: Guidelines and Part 2: Toolbox*, Berlin: YEPP International Resource Centre.

Strocka, C., Duke, P., Engelhardt-Wendt, E., Krüger, A. and Leupold, S. (2009) *Manual for evaluation facilitators, Part 1: Guidelines and Part 2: Toolbox* (2nd edn), Berlin: YEPP International Resource Centre.

Stufflebeam, D. (1988) 'The CIPP model for programme evaluation', in G. Madaus, M. Scriven and D. Stufflebeam (eds) *Evaluation models*, Boston, MA: Kluwer-Nijhoff.

The Innovation Center for Community and Youth Development (2007) *Youth Leadership for Development programme of the USA*, www. theinnovationcenter.org/pdfs/Lessons_in_Leadership exec.pdf.

Tuzla Community Foundation Programme Staff Members (2011) *Tuzla Simin Han and Gornja Tuzla (Bosnia & Herzegovina): The portrait.* Accessible at www.yepp-community.org (10 Years of YEPP/Portraits of Local Sites).

UN Convention on the Rights of the Child (1990), New York: United Nations.

Walther, A. and Pohl, A. (2005) *Thematic study on policy measures concerning disadvantaged youth.* Study commissioned by the European Commission, DG Employment and Social Affairs in the framework of the Community. Action Programme to Combat Social Exclusion 2002–2006. Coordinated by the Institute for Regional Innovation and Social Research (IRIS), Tübingen, Germany, http://ec.europa. eu/employment_social/social_inclusion/docs/youth_study_en.pdf.

Webster, C., MacDonald, R., Shildrick, T. and Simpson, M. (2005) *Social exclusion, young adults and extended youth transitions.* Study by the University of Teesside for the Barrow Cadbury Trust, in P. Bleckmann and A. Krüger, *Youth and community empowerment in practice. Practitioners' handbook based on the concept and the experiences of the Youth Empowerment Partnership Programme*, Berlin: YEPP International Resource Centre, International Academy.

World Bank (2002) *Empowerment and poverty reduction – a source book*, http://siteresources.worldbank.org/INTEMPOWERMENT/ Resources/486312–1095094954594/draft.pdf.

World Bank (2010) *Country classification data*, www.data.worldbank. org/about/country-classification.

World Conference on Community Education (2001) Conference Programme, Vancouver (Canada), p 4.

YEPP (2011) *10 Years of YEPP*, video, www.yepp-community.org.

Index